AN INTRODUCTION TO URBAN DESIGN

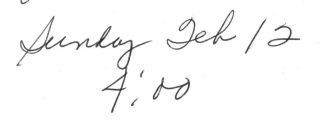

unexpected barriers
for women in Science

Sunday Feb 12
4:00

East Campus Union

AN INTRODUCTION TO URBAN DESIGN

by Jonathan Barnett

ICON EDITIONS

HARPER & ROW, PUBLISHERS, New York
Cambridge, Philadelphia, San Francisco,
London, Mexico City, São Paulo, Sydney

1817

FIRST EDITION

Designer: C. Linda Dingler

Library of Congress Cataloging in Publication Data
Barnett, Jonathan.
　An introduction to urban design.

　(Icon editions)
　Includes index.
　1. City planning.　2. Architecture.　3. Architecture and society.
I. Title.
NA9031.B33 1982　　711′.4　　81-47792
　　　　　　　　　　　　　　AACR2
ISBN 0-06-430376-4　　82 83 84 85 10 9 8 7 6 5 4 3 2 1
ISBN 0-06-430114-1 (pbk) 82 83 84 85 10 9 8 7 6 5 4 3 2 1

Contents

Property owners protest zoning change proposal

Property owners who wish to commercially develop about 4 acres of land near 46th and O streets objected Monday to Planning Director Garner Stoll's recommendation that the area be zoned for apartments.

Part of the area is now zoned for commercial development and some is zoned for lower-density residential use.

Stoll said that zone changes on land to less restrictive uses, which are usually what a developer requests, are part of being a dynamic community.

At the same time, he told City Council members at a public hearing, lines have to be drawn for the public good.

He recommended drawing a line at 201 N. 46th St, where the owners of 2 acres, zoned residential, have requested highway commercial zoning for uses as yet unconfirmed.

That particular zone allows for such uses as small warehouses and auto repair garages and auto sales lots.

According to Stoll, proposing to extend highway commercial zoning northward, off of O Street and onto 46th Street, was an "illogical protusion."

By definition, he said, highway commercial businesses need excellent access and visibility from a major street, which 46th Street is not.

Stoll, supported by the Hartley Neighborhood Association, added that 46th Street will also be more heavily used once the proposed Target and Albertson's Stores northwest of 48th and O street are built.

He said he felt the pocket of land would make an ideal location for an apartment project. He also suggested that more land may become available once nearby Wyuka Cemetary formulates its master plan for growth.

Attorney Mike Rierden, representing the estate of Anna Wentz, which filed for the zone change on 201 N. 46th St, argued it's because of Target and Albertson's that the area will be unsuitable for residential.

Attorney Mark Hunzeker, meanwhile, opposed changing the 2-acre site immediately to the west of 201. N. 46th, which is zoned highway commercial, to apartment zoning also.

Representing the owner and the tenant affected by the change, Sports Courts, Hunzeker told council members that downzoning would decrease the value of the property by an "unconscionable amount."

The council is scheduled to vote on the matter next week.

Editorials

Paul McCue, General Manager, Journal-Star Printing Co.

Tom White........................Editor	William O. Dobler.... Editorial Page Editor
W. Earl Dyer, Jr... Executive Editor	Gordon Winters.....................City Editor

926 P Street, Lincoln 68501   402-473-7301

Unsigned editorials below are the opinion of The Lincoln Star

Tax, Commonwealth occupy first breakfast

At this year's first public breakfast meeting of the Lincoln legislative delegation, the level and equity of taxation and the Commonwealth Savings Co. problem dominated the discussion. The meeting was highlighted with opening remarks by Gov. Bob Kerrey, who impresses us as the most articulate person to occupy the governor's chair in a good long time.

Much of what Kerrey talked about would constitute a good short course in political science. Government is there, he told an overflow crowd, to provide

state takeover and operation of the company. The concern for Commonwealth depositors is just not as great outside Lincoln as it is inside the city, he said.

The governor looked for limited property tax relief in this session of the Legislature, but simply stated that greater property tax equity is "quite another question."

Sen. David Landis of Lincoln addressed the "bombshell" state Supreme Court decision of last Friday

Author's Note

This book started life as an attempt to revise my *Urban Design as Public Policy,* which was published in 1974 and described the experience I and my colleagues had in bringing urban design into the operations of the New York City government. It did not take me long to realize that, in terms of the development of urban design, 1974 was a long time ago, and much of the work described went back further than that. The national experience with urban design was now much broader. My own experience was broader. What I really wanted to do was to write about urban design in more general terms and not restrict myself to New York City. The relatively simple task of revision would not be enough; I needed to write a whole new book.

Readers of the earlier work will recognize some of the material in Chapters 5 and 6, but what I have to say has been changed by subsequent experience. The rest of the book is new, although I have occasionally borrowed a paragraph or two from the earlier text. I hope that the product will be seen to have salvaged those aspects of the earlier work that are still relevant and of general application, and to have integrated this material into a much broader view of urban design, which describes the current state of this rapidly developing art.

New York City
August 18, 1981

PART ONE

THE CHANGING CONTEXT FOR URBAN DESIGN

1

Cities Can
Be Designed

If you believe that cities can be designed, nothing is more frustrating than to watch the continuous misapplication of the huge sums of money that are spent in rebuilding our cities and developing the countryside.

The phrase "developing the countryside" is probably enough to make most people cringe, calling up as it does images of sprawling suburban subdivisions, highway strip development; of fast food shops and auto businesses, billboards, junkyards, mobile home parking clusters, and shopping centers surrounded by huge, desolate parking lots.

Most of us are so used to thinking of these things as a blight on the landscape (although convenient and useful) that we forget how much money has to be expended to make them happen.

Consider highway strip developments. Peter Blake's book *God's Own Junkyard,* * and other subsequent books and articles, have documented their horrors, which of course are visible to most of us every day. As filling stations, supermarkets, and fast food franchises have become a necessary part of our lives, we manage to ignore their aesthetic liabilities. What is so frustrating is that most of these liabilities are unnecessary. Much highway strip development is relatively recent; it all took place over a fairly short time; most of it was financed by highly respectable banks and insurance companies. A little forethought, a little coordination, a

*Peter Blake, *God's Own Junkyard.* New York: Holt, Rinehart & Winston, 1964.

little extra money (but not very much), and it all could have been different.

Consider what happens around a major highway interchange. Let us suppose that you represent a business that is located in another city. You have arrived at your destination late at night, and are staying at a motel located along this highway interchange. To get to your motel you naturally rented an automobile at the airport. The office where you are going for your meeting is within sight of the motel, on the other side of the interchange. You get into your car and drive for several miles along service roads, along a highway in the wrong direction, along more service roads, until you have negotiated the passage between your motel and your appointment. Yes, it would have been faster to walk, except that there are several chain-link fences in your way, and you might well be killed crossing the highway.

Your meeting runs on past lunchtime and you all decide to go out to eat. Someone suggests Captain Ahab's Fish Restaurant, which is located in the parking lot of a shopping center that occupies another quadrant of the same highway interchange. You must all get into cars, drive down service roads, around and back again, to get to your lunch.

The motel, the office building, the shopping center, and the restaurant represent the ingredients of an entire city center. Their location at a highway interchange is entirely rational and predictable. All that was needed was for someone to design their relationships to each other, and to the highways, in a reasonable way. It would probably have saved money; fewer parking places would be needed, less grading, fewer roads.

The same sort of wasteful new development takes place in the older city centers. Four or five new office buildings will be developed within a few years along the same street. There are no connections among them, no shared public spaces, not even provisions to keep them from blocking each other's light.

In a poor neighborhood of the same city, a school, a firehouse, a health service center, and a housing project have been built on the four corners of an intersection. If you stand on one of these corners, every building that

THE CHANGING CONTEXT FOR URBAN DESIGN

you see is new and expensive, but none has any functional or aesthetic connection to any of the others. Each has been built by a different government agency; and there is no more forethought and planning than if each had been built by a separate private investor.

As a last example, consider what happens when a routine street reconstruction takes place. Every city must do street reconstructions; well-administered cities do them every ten to fifteen years. The paving is removed, the bed of the street is relaid or leveled, utility access points are built up or lowered. Often new lampposts, traffic lights, drainage basins, and other street furniture are installed. Then the street is repaved, and *it ends up looking almost exactly the way it did before.*

A large sum of money has been expended. The design value to the city is almost nil.

We are used to talking about a lack of resources as the cause of urban problems, but many of these problems are created by the way we spend the money we have.

Highway interchanges are planned and designed under the direction of government agencies; office buildings, motels and restaurants must all meet local zoning codes. In other words, as a society we are getting what we asked for; why can't we ask for something better? It probably will not cost any more, and it might often cost a great deal less.

It does not take much additional investment to turn a routine street reconstruction into a redesign of the street. Many street patterns are antiquated. In residential areas, streets are often wider than they need to be. More space could be given to trees, to playgrounds, and the same number of parking spaces could be built, just by rearranging the areas devoted to pavement. In city centers, some streets could become malls or transitways, others could have their street lighting improved and sign systems sorted out. If an entire city is scheduled to have street reconstructions done in the course of a generation or less, the whole public environment of the city could be transformed for very little extra money.

The same principle applies in larger questions of public policy relating to the physical environment of the city. Hugh Stretton has observed that ghetto tenants and people who own mobile homes in the United States "pay *more* for their housing over house-hold life than the suburban home-owners do, and have fewer assets in the end."*

*Hugh Stretton, *Urban Planning in Rich and Poor Countries.* New York: Oxford University Press, 1978, p. 150.

There are serious failures and inequities in our society, and they will not disappear even if we learn to make better use of the resources we devote to land development and our public environment. But major improvements are possible within the means we have available today.

What we are talking about is a methodology that helps deal with the accelerated pace of change during our lifetime. Our institutions, and even our understanding, cannot keep up with events. We end up allocating our resources in ways that turn out to be wasteful and illogical.

To judge by the headlines, the urban crisis is last year's problem. So is the environmental crisis, pushed aside by energy and inflation as primary subjects of public concern. But the problems of our cities, the countryside, and the environment in general have not gone away because they are no longer the most popular subjects for television documentaries and newspaper or magazine articles.

There is no escape from these issues, as the people who sought a self-sufficient life-style in remote rural areas have discovered. The traditional distinctions between city and suburb, or between rural and urban areas, have been obliterated by the growth and change of the last few decades.

There is general acceptance of the need to deal with urban and environmental problems if ways can be found to do so. There is a new public understanding of ecology—the relatedness of the actions that affect the environment. We have acquired a newly conservative attitude toward both nature and buildings, a suspicion of proposals that purport to be improvements, a resistance to large-scale plans. Where once people assumed that change was both necessary and desirable, now they

THE CHANGING CONTEXT FOR URBAN DESIGN

may take it for granted that anything new is going to be a disaster. The result: a new emphasis on community participation and review, and an increased popularity for historic preservation.

Design is a methodology that, when applied to public policy, can help solve some of the problems of misallocated resources, misused land, and the unnecessary destruction of historic buildings. The process of designing a house allocates resources and resolves conflicts. You shouldn't need to go through the bedrooms to get from the dining room to the kitchen; the overall shape of the house should be economical; the structural and mechanical systems should make sense, but be subordinate to the rooms. You don't expect to see heating pipes in front of the doors that lead to the garden. In a hospital, you don't expect each element to have its own building, with separate roads and parking lots connecting the X-ray department with the emergency room, and the surgical suite, although admittedly some hospitals are a little like that.

A city is far more complex than even the most complicated building, but there are ways of introducing into our cities some of the coherence and even beauty that are the products of design. The working methods shown in this book are specific and practicable. They are accompanied by examples, so that the reader can decide whether they represent an improvement.

We start with the assumption that we cannot afford to write off the very substantial investment—social, financial, and cultural—in the existing fabric of our cities. Perhaps this seems an obvious and unnecessary assertion, although it does not seem to be taken for granted in debates about the financial future of New York or Cleveland or the "Sun Belt" versus the "Frost Belt." In addition, many of the widely publicized concepts about designing cities start from the opposite premise.

What is called the Modern movement in architecture has tended to advocate wiping out existing cities and replacing them with something more rational and hygienic. The French-Swiss architect Le Corbusier, in his famous Voisin Plan for obliterating Paris, produced what is perhaps the most widely remembered image of modern town planning. Only Notre Dame and a few other historic buildings would have survived. The studies of the Congrès International de l'Architecture Moderne (CIAM) had a rather similar intent.

Le Corbusier's Voisin Plan for Paris: writing off the city and starting over again.

These polemics against existing cities have been very influential in ways that their authors did not foresee. What began as a romantic vision of modern technology, freeing the individual from the constraints of tradition, has turned out to be admirably suited to mindless bureaucratic repetition, and the cost cutting of profit-motivated entrepreneurs. The inhumane environment and stereotyped design that critics like Jane Jacobs have so justly criticized in the average urban renewal project are a direct consequence of this "modernist" concept of the city.

The modern city, and the modern social organization of which it is a part, are clearly far more subtle and complex than the revolutionary vision of sixty years ago had recognized.

Unfortunately, architects and planners have too often reacted to the evident failure of their theories about cities not by revising their theories but by condemning society, and by indulging in escapist fantasies.

It is amazing how many texts on urban design confine themselves to the questions that concerned city designers in the eighteenth century: the enclosure of plazas and streets, the axis, the vista, the progression. These issues are important, and it is true that the "modernists" very foolishly ignored them; but there are many design problems in today's cities where these traditional concepts are not much help.

THE CHANGING CONTEXT FOR URBAN DESIGN

Another form of escapism is a rush to embrace a future in which everything will be mechanized, and communication will be both instantaneous and total. Designers have spent their time portraying cities as walking pods, spherical honeycombs, or endlessly spreading "space frames." Aside from the fact that such proposals ignore our existing inventory of cities, the social structure necessary to make such futuristic visions work would be the most regressive imaginable.

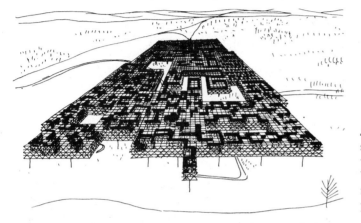

Spatial City by Yona Friedman. A spreading space-frame housing all urban activities which would replace the conventional city. What kind of social structure would be needed to permit this transformation to take place?

Planners take refuge in diagrams so abstract that the rational future they portray is completely removed from current property values or everyday decision making. Others evade the issue of improving cities by resisting change of any kind, or by seeking to duplicate life as it was in pre-industrial times. An even more subtle form of escape is to say that cities are the expression of the society that created them, and there is therefore no hope for cities until society is reformed.

Certainly no one who has lived in the slums of our cities, or has talked to and worked with the people who live in them, can have much satisfaction about the way our society works today. Each designer or planner must decide how to respond to this situation. But making physical improvements in cities is a process intimately connected to the social and power structures, and it is in the area of physical conservation or change that people trained as designers are most likely to have a useful contribution to make.

Today's city is not an accident. Its form is usually

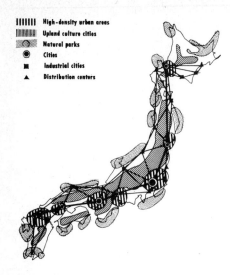

Urban areas |||||||| Development areas |||||||||| Upland culture cities   Natural parks
— — — Roads   ········ High-speed trunk railway lines   ◉ Regional growth poles   ● New towns

Above: a master plan for the Japanese Archipelago, to be attained by the year 2000. At this level of abstraction, answers to urban problems look simpler than they really are.

Above right: a master plan for the Tokyo region and, opposite, a detail of one district within the plan. The real problems involve implementation, and the creation of a humane environment within such a plan.

unintentional, but it is not accidental. It is the product of decisions made for single, separate purposes, whose interrelationships and side effects have not been fully considered. The design of cities has been determined by engineers, surveyors, lawyers, and investors, each making individual, rational decisions for rational reasons, but leaving the design of the city to be taken care of later, if at all.

Cities are not designed by making pictures of the way they should look twenty years from now. They are created by a decision-making process that goes on continuously, day after day. If people trained as designers are to influence the shape of the city, they need both a strong vision of what ought to happen and the opportunity to be present when the critical decisions are being made.

People of importance in government and real estate are used to considering "design" as the icing on the cake. At the same time, they are often strongly in-

THE CHANGING CONTEXT FOR URBAN DESIGN

fluenced by design ideas that they do not really understand, and that come to them in garbled form. The design professional is at least partly to blame for having such an ineffective role in the design of cities.

Architects and planners have inherited some funny ideas about themselves as the keepers of the sacred flame of culture and the guardians of society's conscience. There has been a tradition that a true professional and, certainly, a true artist, should not be too closely involved in the day-to-day process of government, or politics, or real estate development. Instead, architects and planners have sent instructions to the policymakers as manifestos or visionary drawings; and, not surprisingly, the policymakers find them impossibly idealistic and irrelevant to the problem at hand. At the same time, because ideas like the city of towers in a park or advocacy planning are such strong concepts, they eventually work their way into the decision-making

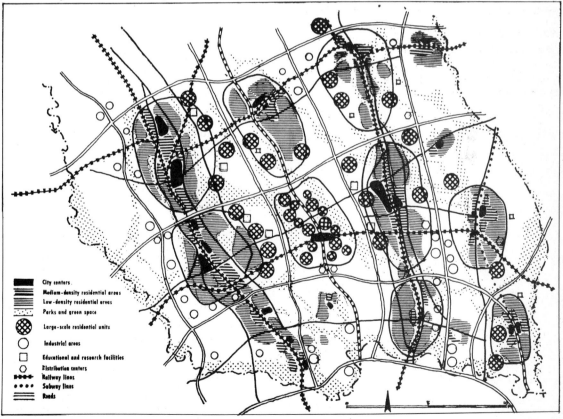

City centers
Medium-density residential areas
Low-density residential areas
Parks and green space
Large-scale residential units
Industrial areas
Educational and research facilities
Distribution centers
Railway lines
Subway lines
Roads

process, but seldom in the form their authors intended.

Fortunately, the architectural and planning professions have now come to recognize that they must take an active rather than a purely advisory role. The day-to-day decisions about the allocation of government money according to conflicting needs and different political interests, or the economics of real estate investment, are in fact the medium of city design, as essential to the art as paint to the painter. To produce significant results, from both a practical and an artistic point of view, urban designers must rid themselves of the notion that their work will be contaminated by an understanding of political and real estate decisions. It is not always necessary to approve; it is essential to understand.

The process of making an urban design concept politically viable or economically feasible may give an unexpected, but valuable, assist to the design process itself. It may even change the nature of the design objectives. In the words of the old Cunard slogan, "getting there is half the fun," and who can be sure of a destination that is fifteen or twenty years away?

Instead of handing over city designs or policy positions as an ostensibly finished product, designers of cities should seek to write the rules for the significant choices that shape the city, within an institutional framework that can be modified as times, and needs, change. That institutional framework should include the designer, who must be part of the decision-making process in order to be effective.

Urban design is the generally accepted name for the process of giving physical design direction to urban growth, conservation, and change. It is understood to include landscape as well as buildings, both preservation and new construction, and rural areas as well as cities. Many people have tried to find a new term that would make this inclusivity more obvious, but it is easier, and more productive, to go on using an accepted term than to educate everyone to use a different description. After all, Buick is not all that good a name for a motorcar, but it acquired the right meaning through usage.

The development of urban design as a separate technical specialty is relatively recent, but it has been rapid. The first academic curriculum in the United States was the University of Pennsylvania's Civic Design Program, begun in 1957, followed by Harvard's Urban Design Program in 1960. Now it is offered at dozens of universities either as a degree program or as an area of concentration within architecture or city planning.

I run a graduate program in urban design myself at the City College of New York. Since we began the program in 1971, I don't believe we have ever taught a course the same way two years in a row. Each year new books appear, new examples are available, new techniques have been developed.

When I and my colleagues went to work for the New York City Planning Department in 1967, answering the telephone by saying "Urban Design Group" seemed in itself to be a radical act; now people with urban design titles are routinely employed in cities and counties, at planning departments and development agencies. The private practice of urban design has grown from a handful of specialists to the point where there are probably as many urban design jobs in the private sector as there are in government.

In 1967 successful recent examples of urban design were few and hard to find. Today, almost every element of the city has been designed successfully somewhere, although these elements have never been put together in one place. There is solid evidence that a designed city is more than a presumption.

The first part of this book is devoted to the changing political context for urban design: environmental conservation, community participation, and historic preservation.

Much of the recent history of urban design has been concerned with the problem of designing cities without designing buildings, the subject of the second section of the book. If development controls are too architecturally explicit too soon, they cannot be followed and they fail. If development controls are too general, they also fail. Chapter 5 summarizes the traditional methods of controlling urban design through zoning, mapping, and urban renewal. The next two chapters describe New

York City's efforts to improve upon these traditional methods through special zoning measures. The following chapter is devoted to a parallel effort in San Francisco, and the section concludes with descriptions of design methods for planned communities.

The last part of the book deals with urban design methodology. A land-use strategy for conservation, growth, and change is essential. There should be a public open-space plan that pulls together outdoor and indoor spaces that are open to the public, including streets—which should not be considered leftover areas, but a basis for the design of many components of the city. Street design requires standards for street lighting, street graphics, and street furniture. There should also be a mechanism for making transportation decisions part of the city design concept. Development controls, whose evolution is described in Part Two, are a major implementation mechanism, as is the strategic use of public investment, the subject of the final chapter.

There is an Afterword on the urban design profession.

Again, no claims are advanced that urban design is a cure-all. It ought to be self-evident, but somehow is not, that cities cannot solve their problems without the aid of national housing, employment, welfare, and education policies. These ideas are not fashionable at present, when the federal government is seen as doing too much already. No doubt there are many governmental activities that can benefit from stronger local control; but, without a national policy context, those cities that are doing relatively well simply become a magnet to people from less fortunate places, and the gains are offset by new problems.

Nevertheless, it is still sound policy to do what we can right now. The answers to many difficult urban situations are like destinations at the end of a winding road. It is not always clear where we are headed; but if we do not set out, we will never arrive.

THE CHANGING CONTEXT FOR URBAN DESIGN

2

Environmental Design and Environmental Conservation

"The Congress, recognizing the profound impact of man's activity on the interrelations of all components of the natural environment. . . ." So begins Title One of the National Environmental Policy Act of 1969, which announced a significant change in the way our government makes decisions.

Rachel Carson's popular *Silent Spring,* first published in 1962, may have been the most important single means of creating public recognition that our species occupies a place in the natural order. We have been able to assert so much power over the environment that we had forgotten we were a part of it. Nature will always reach a natural equilibrium; the problem was to make us realize that we could bring about an equilibrium that does not include ourselves.

The decade of the 1960s saw a huge shift in public opinion away from "Who cares about a few birds?" to "We'd better do something before it's too late." The 1969 act, known familiarly as NEPA, contains extraordinarily sweeping language, and its full effect has yet to be felt.

Under the act, all agencies of the federal government shall "utilize a systematic, interdisciplinary approach which will insure the integrated use of the natural and social sciences and the environmental design arts in planning and decisionmaking which may have an impact on man's environment. . . ." Note the words, "envi-

Environmental Impact Analysis Mandates Urban Design

ronmental design arts." It was a new situation for "urban design," to be mandated by the federal government.

The major practical effect of NEPA has been to require a detailed statement by the "responsible official" in every recommendation or report about proposed legislation or other major federal actions "significantly affecting the quality of the human environment." This report must describe:

(i) the environmental impact of the proposed action,

(ii) any adverse environmental effects which cannot be avoided should the proposal be implemented,

(iii) alternatives to the proposed action,

(iv) the relationship between local short-term uses of man's environment and the maintenance and enhancement of long-term productivity, and

(v) any irreversible and irretrievable commitments of resources which would be involved in the proposed action should it be implemented.

The procedure required by NEPA has come to be called an Environmental Impact Statement. However, there is nothing in the act that sets standards for acceptable or unacceptable environmental impacts. Technically, a statement could find that the proposed action would bring about the end of life on earth as we know it, and the agency could still go right ahead. There is also nothing in the act that sets standards of adequacy for such statements. It is up to the "responsible official," ordinarily the Secretary of a federal department or the head of an agency, to set the administrative standards. On the other hand, a member of the public who does not feel that the standards are adequate can always bring a lawsuit and ask the courts to decide whether the Environmental Impact Statement was sufficiently thorough to comply with NEPA. The stage is thus set for two major problems with the administration of this act: we can call them the Environmental Impact Neurosis and the environmental hostage.

While the intentions of the National Environmental Policy Act and other such legislation were totally admirable, they set standards for the natural and social sciences, and for design and public policy, that were way ahead of current knowledge and practice. There are many other federal laws dealing with environmental issues that set similar requirements. Some are concerned with protecting resources, such as wetlands, coastal zones, or agricultural and forest land; others regulate sources of pollution, such as the laws dealing with air and water quality and hazardous waste disposal. Federal highway legislation not only mandates Environmental Impact Statements but requires that land-use and urban design issues be considered in the initial planning of the highway.

Biology and environmental sciences have made great strides, but we are a long way from a full, systematic understanding of how our natural environment works. The social sciences generate a vast literature, but the interactions of society are hardly well understood either. When we are required by law to estimate the effect of the interactions between natural and social systems, we can only make educated guesses.

The Environmental Neurosis

This is where the Environmental Impact Neurosis begins. If you have ever sat up in bed and asked yourself: "Did I lock the front door?", you may have experienced the neurotic sequence of thoughts that I am describing as akin to environmental impact procedures. You get up to check the door, which is indeed locked, and then, when you are back in bed, you begin to wonder: "When I checked the door, did I leave the light on in the front hall?" After you have checked the light, you wonder: "When I locked the door, was the cat in or out?", which requires opening the door again; and so on. It is hard to finish an Environmental Impact Statement, because the process is so much of an institutionalized neurosis; there is no end to the questions that might plausibly be investigated.

The Environmental Hostage

The snail darter is a small fish that became widely known some years ago because it was an environmental hostage. There was a dispute as to whether the snail darter in question was a separate species; whether—if it were—the species would be endangered by the construction of a dam; and if it were endangered, whether the danger was significant. The opponents of the dam were not particularly interested in the snail darter, but

*While it was the NEPA procedure that raised the snail darter issue, it was the Endangered Species Act, before Congress amended it, that created an obstacle to building the dam.

†For an account of some pioneering state environmental regulations, see *The Quiet Revolution in Land Use Control* by Fred Bosselman and David Callies. Washington, D.C: Council on Environmental Quality, 1971.

it was a convenient issue for trying to stop construction. The NEPA procedure is capable of creating an infinite number of these issues.* It is not that environmental conservatism isn't a sound policy; rather, environmental conservatism has created a major shift in the way government decisions are made, and there is a strong element of plausible nonsense in many of these environmental disputes because our knowledge does not begin to live up to the standards set by the law.

Many states now have environmental impact regulations of their own, and probably all of them will in time.† These regulations cover not only the actions of state governments but often privately financed projects that are big enough to come under the criteria of the law. For example, in Florida, the Environmental Land and Water Management Act of 1972 requires a review and approval process for all developments of regional impact. Such a development was defined in the act as that which, "because of its character, magnitude and location would have a substantial effect upon the health, safety and or welfare of citizens of more than one county." The state later legislated administrative standards for evaluating Developments of Regional Impact—known as DRIs—that are applicable to airports, tourist attractions and recreation facilities, electrical generating facilities and transmission lines, hospitals, industrial plants and industrial parks, mining operations, office parks, petroleum storage facilities, port facilities, residential developments, schools, and shopping centers.

A developer or agency which finds that a project is defined as having regional impact must submit an application to the local government that would have jurisdiction in any case, to one of the seven regional planning agencies that are designated to administer the act, and to the Division of State Planning. The regional planning agency prepares an advisory report, but it is the local planning agency that actually makes the decision. There is the possibility of an appeal to the Florida Land and Water Adjudicatory Commission, which is actually the governor and cabinet. Thus the state has an opportunity to override a local deci-

THE CHANGING CONTEXT FOR URBAN DESIGN

sion. Of course, there is always a possibility of an appeal to the courts.*

Under both federal and state environmental regulations, a lot of development that we see every day would not be possible if it were to be proposed now. The apartment towers next to the highway, the routine draining of swamps and bulldozing of hillsides, the hotel perched on sand dunes may no longer meet environmental standards. The environmental process has thus improved the way development is done, but it has its negative side.

The Environmental Impact Statement that is produced to fulfill these new requirements is a long and complex document. First, the development must be described in objective language and great detail, and the existing context for development must be described, again in great detail. The categories of environmental impact include the natural environment, impact upon the economic and social context of the project, as well as such traditional planning considerations as public facilities, land use, parking, and transportation. The natural environment can, in turn, be subdivided into issues of air and water quality, the preservation of habitats and species of both flora and fauna, geologic issues, and the overall natural equilibrium. Social and economic issues have almost endless ramifications, and can involve the authors of the statement in speculation, indeed, in fiction. What is the economic impact of a proposal that diverts a small percentage of the traffic on a commercial street to one that is more residential in character? Does business on the commercial street suffer? Do property values on the residential street go down? If so, are the changes significant? Does a small economic impact of a negative kind balance the preservation of an existing habitat by diverting the traffic? In any event, the unavoidable adverse environmental effects, no matter how speculative they may be, must be catalogued in the statement.

The requirement to consider alternatives to proposed actions sounds reasonable but can create terrible problems. How seriously must the alternatives be considered? Does each require the same level of detail as the

*See Robert M. Rhodes, "DRIs and Florida's Land Development Policies," in *Florida Environmental and Urban Issues,* Vol. II, no. 3, pp. 5 ff.

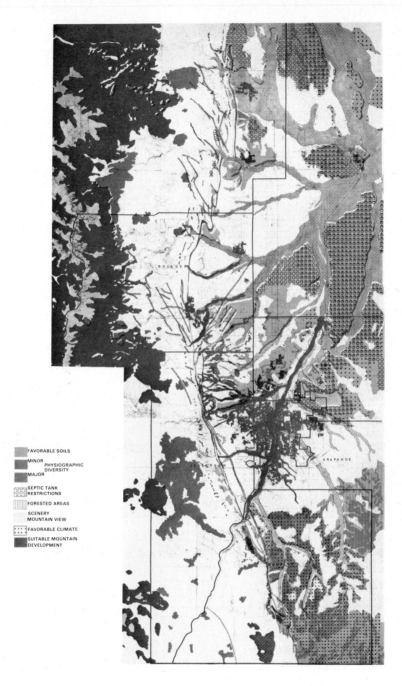

FAVORABLE SOILS

MINOR
        PHYSIOGRAPHIC
        DIVERSITY
MAJOR

SEPTIC TANK
RESTRICTIONS

FORESTED AREAS

SCENERY
MOUNTAIN VIEW

FAVORABLE CLIMATE

SUITABLE MOUNTAIN
DEVELOPMENT

A map of the region just to the east of the Rocky Mountains to the north and south of Denver, Colorado, by Wallace, McHarg, Roberts & Todd, showing the areas where the "concurrence of all propitious factors combined with the absence of all detrimental ones constitutes the highest fitness for urban land use."

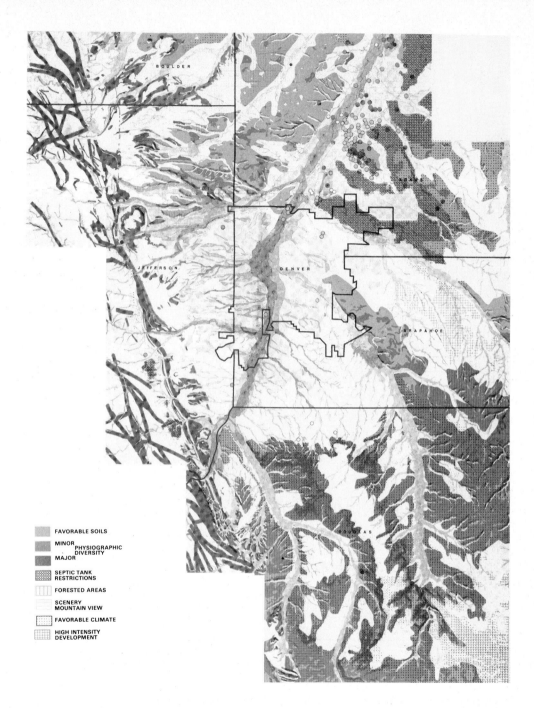

FAVORABLE SOILS

MINOR
PHYSIOGRAPHIC
DIVERSITY
MAJOR

SEPTIC TANK
RESTRICTIONS

FORESTED AREAS

SCENERY
MOUNTAIN VIEW

FAVORABLE CLIMATE

HIGH INTENSITY
DEVELOPMENT

A map of the Denver metropolitan region that is essentially a more detailed version of the map on the opposite page. These two maps were developed as part of a planning study for rapid transit in the Denver area.

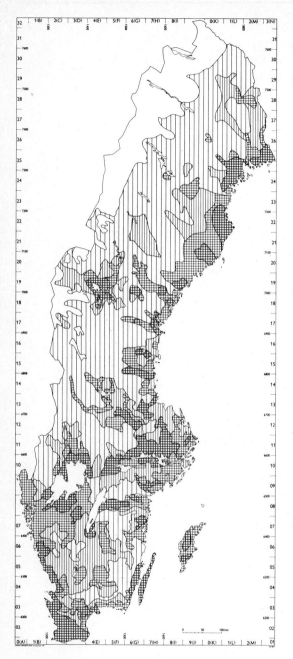

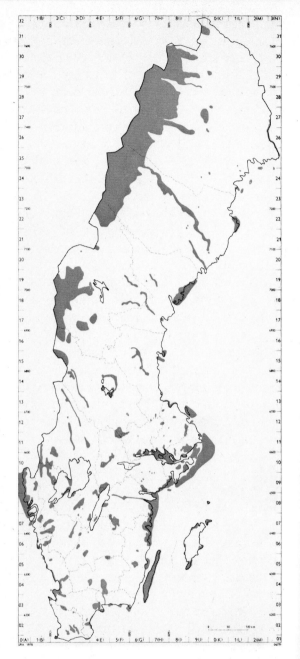

A map from a national planning study of Sweden, which shows the ecological basis for separating forestry from other agricultural uses.

Another map from the same planning study, showing major areas of national interest for open-air recreation.

THE CHANGING CONTEXT FOR URBAN DESIGN

real proposal, which would triple or quadruple the planning costs? Should the statement discuss only real alternatives that were seriously considered or the full range of potential actions? What are the trade-offs between short- and long-term considerations that, under the law, must be considered? What constitutes an irreversible and irretrievable commitment of resources? Are we talking about construction or long-term operation? And so on. The process raises endless questions, and elicits lengthy documents that few people can be expected to actually read.

The most disturbing aspect of the environmental analyses that are now required by law is that they deal with regional issues on a local, case-by-case basis. A proposed hospital may have to go through an environmental impact analysis; so will the shopping center across the highway and the office park on the hill behind. Obviously a great deal of trouble would be saved, and a better job of conserving and adapting the environment would be done, if all three projects were to be considered as part of a more comprehensive process. Environmental impact analysis also has a way of superseding existing land-use controls, which continue to apply to small projects but not to big ones. Land may be zoned for high-intensity development and then found to be wetlands, which should not be disturbed.

The logical alternative would seem to be some kind of regional environmental zoning. The authorities would take on the burden of stating what development would be acceptable, and the cost of environmental investigation would not have to be borne by individual projects. There is only one small problem with this kind of logic. It involves planners saying to federal agencies or to the governor and legislature: "We have just thought of a way of taking every environmental controversy that might occur in the next twenty years and having all these fights right now." Most people in public life would not regard this as a favor.

Even if there were the political will to overcome the redundancies and illogicalities of environmental impact analysis, we need a more systematic method for documenting and evaluating these issues.

Ian McHarg's *Design with Nature* (for a more complete description of McHarg's theories, see page 140) provides one way of putting the relationships between people and their environment onto a more systematic basis. The sequence of environmental maps, which are overlaid to exclude the sensitive parts of the ecosystem from development, provides a sound, objective basis for regional environmental zoning, particularly in areas where there has been little development up to now.

Another promising method of objectifying environmental considerations can be found in Howard T. Odum's book, *Environment, Power and Society,* first published in 1971.* Odum takes systems analysis techniques that were devised for mechanical and electrical engineering, as well as to help design industrial production methods, and applies them to natural systems—and even to social systems. One of the by-products of Odum's book is that he is able to make the connection between natural systems and their economic value in our society. He gives as an example a controversy in North Carolina where a right of way was to be cut through a forested public park. The state officials

*New York: Wiley Interscience, 1971.

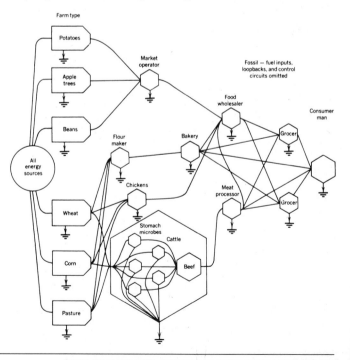

A diagram from Howard T. Odum's *Environment, Power and Society,* showing the loss of power through convergence of food chains necessary to develop quality nutrition.

THE CHANGING CONTEXT FOR URBAN DESIGN

valued the damage to the public on a per acre basis as $64, the value of the wood they cut. Odum took a different basis for his calculation: the cost of replacing the forest, which would take one hundred years. He calculated the energy required for the photosynthesis that would produce the forest, then estimated its dollar equivalent in energy derived from fossil fuels. In pre-OPEC dollars, Odum valued each acre of forest at $590,000, each mature tree at about $3,000.

Odum gives analogous calculations that show how much energy is produced by each acre of a wetlands system and what its equivalent economic value would be. Such energy accounting would be a useful means of estimating whether various environmental impacts were socially acceptable or not.

I have not given an adequate synopsis of either McHarg's or Odum's books because I have concentrated on the immediate applicability of their work to the current defiencies of environmental impact studies. Both books embody much of their author's life work, and have a strong philosophical component; both build theories on the scientific work of many other people. My own view is that the physical and environmental implications of McHarg's and Odum's theories are more convincing than some of their general social speculations.

A combination of environmental zoning, objective accounting systems for environmental values, and the methods of objectifying design quality through legislation that are described in Part Two of this book and in Chapter 14 would make it possible for environmental regulations to live up to the high expectations already set for them by Congress and state legislatures.

The Positive Value of Limits

The recognition that there are limits to growth and that natural resources are becoming scarcer has positive value from an environmental point of view. The positive effect created by the energy crisis is that using less fossil fuel, reducing the development potential of outlying suburbs, and re-using existing resources all strengthen the possibility of creating more responsible ways of developing our surroundings.

A graphic representation of natural resource issues from the Environmental Impact Statement for the Gateway National Recreation Area in New York City.

Economic necessity should reinforce political will, making it easier to adopt more workable environmental regulations as the professionals find ways of creating them.

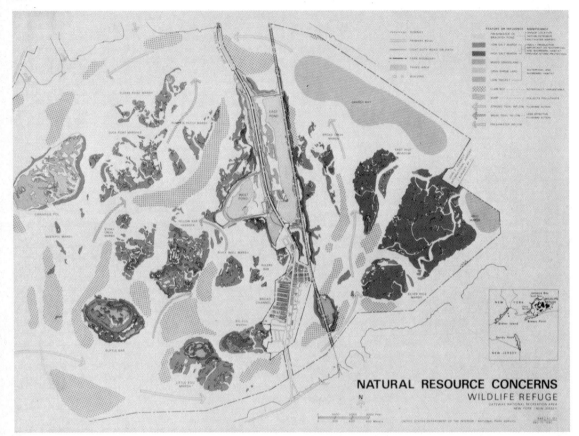

NATURAL RESOURCE CONCERNS

WILDLIFE REFUGE

3

Community Participation in Urban Design Decisions

The ideal pattern for American local government is the town meeting, in which all important decisions are made in public and every citizen has a voice.

Although the town meeting still exists in many localities, our big cities have grown a long way from this kind of direct democracy. Citizens seldom have any idea how and when important decisions are made, much less any knowledge of how to influence them, even if they are of immediate concern. The first intimation that many a local resident has had of an impending highway or housing project has been the arrival of the surveyors —or an eviction notice.

A system of notification in obscure journals of record and the mystifying procedures and calendars of public hearings have given a cloak of popular consent to some highly arbitrary actions, particularly when these actions have been taken by independent authorities or entrenched governmental bureaucracies, which are a long way from being responsive to the voters.

The result has too often been a confrontation between angry citizens and well-established plans that have developed past the point where meaningful change is possible. If the plans go through, the citizens are left with a sense of helpless anger and alienation. If the plans are stopped, nothing may happen for years, and government becomes powerless and ineffective.

Community participation in planning offers an alternative to the demonstrated ineffectiveness of the city planner who operated from outside the political process on the basis of superior professional knowledge of what was good for the public. Enough such plans had been carried out, particularly in the area of urban renewal and highways, that the public had become deeply—and legitimately—distrustful of planners, and was learning how to organize demonstrations of opposition in order to stop their plans.

Paul Davidoff, a city planner who is also a lawyer, suggested in an article published in 1965* that planning should be modeled on the legal system. Every interest in the community should have its own planner and plans, and truth would emerge through an adversary process, as it is meant to do in a court of law.

*"Advocacy and Pluralism in Planning," *Journal of the American Institute of Planners* (November 1965), pp. 331ff.

The idea of this kind of "advocacy planning" enjoyed a considerable vogue during the late 1960s, although it never was clear who was to function as either judge or jury. In cases where the official local government is completely unresponsive to a community, advocacy planning is both necessary and an effective means of communication; but as a general method of planning for the future, it seems more likely to produce controversy than results.

An alternative method of community participation, developed at about the same time, calls for representatives of all the interest groups affected by a plan to be formed into a working committee. A professional then creates a rational structure for the issues and leads the working group to a consensus that becomes the plan.

This method might be called the gospel according to Archibald Rogers, a Baltimore architect who has promoted the idea of working committees and "urban design concept teams" with evangelical fervor.

†See Jonathan Barnett, "A Planning Process with Built-In Political Support," in *Architectural Record* (May 1966).

Rogers had evolved his theories while developing the plan for downtown Cincinnati.† Between 1961 and 1963, Cincinnati had tried three of the conventional ways to arrive at a downtown renewal plan, and all of them had failed. The proposal drawn by Cincinnati's own city planning department had been shelved by the City Council over the issue of an underground garage

THE CHANGING CONTEXT FOR URBAN DESIGN

and circulation system. A study of the city core by Victor Gruen Associates, which had been commissioned by a group representing downtown business and financial interests, was not accepted because it proposed closing a number of streets. A third study, drawn by Barton–Aschman Associates on behalf of the real estate group that had been selected as developers, was also unable to win approval. That left the city of Cincinnati with a loan and grant application pending in Washington, a redeveloper already selected and financing assured, and no agreement on the design plan to be followed.

The way out of the impasse was suggested by Herbert W. Stevens, who was then Cincinnati's planning director. In May of 1963, he wrote to the City Manager:

It will be a waste of time to work on a new plan without a process for resolving differences, step by step, before the work has crystallized into proposals.

Consequently, a process should be established whereby the City Planning Commission and City Council can work together, step by step, in creating a new plan which will lead up a ladder of planning decisions until a plan is developed which will be acceptable to both sides. The ladder of planning decisions would become an educational process, as well as a decision-making process.

The letter went on to propose that a working committee be established composed of representatives from the City Council, the City Planning Commission, and the Downtown Development Committee.

Archibald Rogers and his firm, RTKL, were retained to make a fresh start, along with transportation and economic consultants. A strong chairman was found for the working review committee; and consultants and the committee began a series of meetings that took place every two weeks. It was agreed as procedure that each step in the planning process would be programmed as a series of decisions, which would be voted on by the working review committee. In the interval between meetings, the decisions were to be ratified by the City Council and City Planning Commission. As working majorities of both bodies were represented on

Cross Reference		Decision	Explanatory Comments
	G.	Block H	
p. 4, I. A. 2. p. 10, I. A. 11	1.	Predominant Use: Predominant parking use with possibility for retail at grade. Expansion of block to include northwest corner.	The original boundary for Block H only included the northeast corner. The planners recommended an expansion of the block west along Sixth Street in order to provide an adequate site for an efficient self-park garage. The Working Review Committee accepted this expansion during the April 9, 1964 meeting.
pp. 10-13, I. A. 12	2.	Program of Space and Use	

a.1) Low-rate parking - 800 cars.

III.G.2.a. was recommended 4/9/64 as the design assumption for the development of Block H in relation to the remainder of the CBD.

2) Retail - up to 50,000 square feet.

	'64-'69	'70-'75	'76-'85	Total
b. Parking		600 sp.		600 sp.

III.G.2.b. is the revised program of space and use recommended 7/29/64 reflecting the design and market analysis made during the period between 4/9/64 and 7/29/64. This supersedes III.G.2.a. and should therefore be used, since it expressed the most definite program goal.

Cross Reference		Decision	Explanatory Comments
	3.	Basic Organization:	
p. 104, IV. A. 3.		a. The opportunity for retailing if exploited, shall be oriented toward Walnut Street and toward the pedestrian traffic movement mentioned in III.G.6.a.	The Walnut Street orientation faces Block A and the Sixth Street orientation would recognize the east-west pedestrian movement along Sixth Street.
		b. Efforts shall be made to provide retail space on the ground level of the parking facility facing Sixth Street.	
p. 19, I. C. 4. p. 26, II. A. 9.	7.	Off-street truck service shall be provided for the facilities in the block.	
	8.	Approximate size of the block shall be:	

North-South   350'
East-West   390'
136,000 square feet for private development.

Text of decisions made as a part of the downtown Cincinnati plan.
Cross-references are to other related decisions in other parts of the plan. The form in which decisions were made permitted them to be adopted by the Planning Commission and the City Council as the planning process took place.

the committee, such ratification was expected. If it was not forthcoming, the matter was to be referred back to the working review committee. Each meeting took two days, the first for presentation by the consultants, the second for discussion and decision.

The final plan exists as a series of some 250 city ordinances that vary from expressions of philosophical intent to specific statements governing the width of sidewalks. In this way a planning process was created that builds in both political support and an implementation procedure.

Archibald Rogers had defined the steps in this urban design and planning process by a military analogy:

SURVEY

Stage 1 is reconnaissance, a general survey of the existing situation.

GOALS

Stage 2 is the selection of a series of strategic objectives.

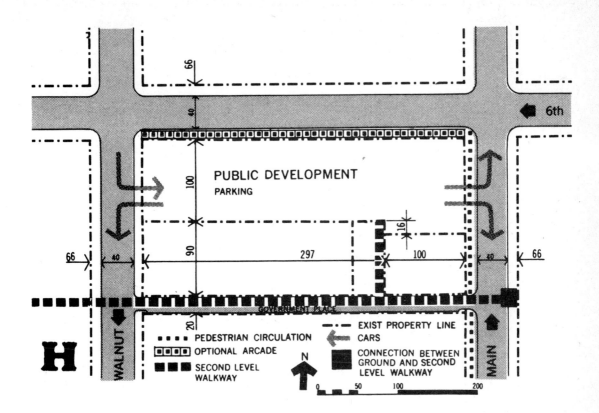

Within the figure:

66

40

6th ←

PUBLIC DEVELOPMENT
PARKING

100

16

90   297   100   40   66

66   40

20

GOVERNMENT PLACE

H

WALNUT

MAIN

N

•••• PEDESTRIAN CIRCULATION
☐☐☐☐ OPTIONAL ARCADE
■■■ SECOND LEVEL
      WALKWAY

—·— EXIST PROPERTY LINE
←   CARS
■   CONNECTION BETWEEN
    GROUND AND SECOND
    LEVEL WALKWAY

0   50   100   200

Stage 3 is the consideration and selection of alternative
   strategies to achieve the objectives.
Stage 4, which is tactics, is the design process itself.

Rogers went on to use the procedure elsewhere; other
planners and designers learned from his experience; and
something like the Cincinnati format, a working review
committee and a four-stage decision-making process,
has now become standard practice.

There have also been some experiments with putting
such a planning process on television, with people able
to call in suggestions and see plans modified immediately. For meaningful community participation in plans
that cover a large region, some form of televised planning clearly makes a lot of sense.

However, most planning proposals involve a small
constituency and a limited geographic area. In these

This map of Block H in downtown
Cincinnati shows in graphic form the
decisions outlined on the opposite page.

31

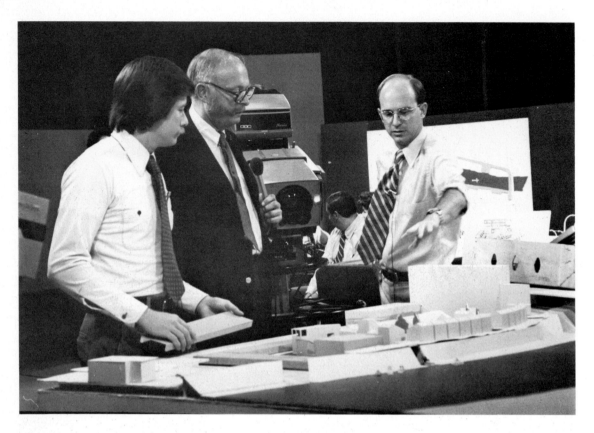

A photograph taken during a televised "designathon," which was part of the planning process for the Dayton, Ohio, riverfront in 1976. From left to right: Steven Carter of the Dayton firm of Lorenz & Williams, and Charles Moore and Chad Floyd of Moore, Grover, Harper, the urban design and architectural consultants. In response to comments telephoned in by viewers, the urban designers are showing different building alternatives within a site model of the downtown riverfront.

instances, the working committee is the key to whether community participation will be successful or not.

The Cincinnati experience turned out to be somewhat misleading to those of us who attempted to apply it in other situations. In Cincinnati, the committee chairman had been Mark Upson, a retired top executive at Proctor and Gamble, who did not have a direct personal stake in the controversies surrounding the plan but was known and respected by everyone. Upson also was experienced in running meetings, and knew how to get groups to come to an agreement.

An Upson-like figure is essential in any planning process that uses a working review committee, and such people are not always available. The planning or design consultant is always perceived as an outsider, and cannot take over the chairman's role.

The Cincinnati working committee had unquestionable legitimacy because it included City Council mem-

THE CHANGING CONTEXT FOR URBAN DESIGN

bers, members of the Planning Commission, and business leaders who controlled the property most likely to be affected by the plan. Committee members were also used to making group decisions and trading one set of interests off against another.

When some of us attempted to apply the Cincinnati methods to local neighborhoods in New York City, we found that a legitimate working committee was difficult to create, and it took a long time for a leader to emerge who could run a meeting in an orderly way and keep it to the point.

Sometimes it proved impossible to create a single working group; in such cases it was necessary for the planners and designers to shuttle back and forth between several different community organizations.

How can one be sure that a community group does legitimately represent a real constituency? It is very difficult.

A working committee can be elected, but these kinds of unofficial elections are generally not taken seriously by a majority of the voters. Government officials should be cautious about appointing a committee, however, since even if all factions are represented, such committees can be regarded as a put-up job. Some of the most successful committees just form themselves, strange as this may seem. Inevitably, some people will be overlooked, or will not take the effort seriously. Before the conventional public hearing, it is worth holding local hearings in the community to pick up the people who have been left out and to ratify the decisions of the working group. If the working committee is a good one, its members will help marshall community support for its plans.

If at all possible, the government officials concerned with implementing the plan should be represented while the committee is meeting, as it is not much use to arrive at a consensus in the community if the government is not going to follow it.

The planning process in the working committee should begin by reaching agreement on a description of existing conditions in the neighborhood. Sometimes a local resident, following customary routes through the

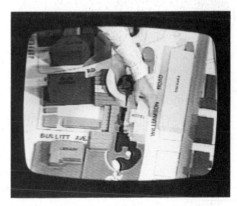

These photographs, taken from television screens, show what viewers saw during presentations of downtown planning alternatives for Roanoke, Virginia, in 1979. Top: the telephone panel taking questions and the number viewers should call. Bottom: a change being made in response to a viewer's suggestion. The hand belongs to Chad Floyd of Moore, Grover, Harper.

area for years, will be ignorant of conditions right around the block from home. On the other hand, planning and design professionals, who are outsiders, may draw the wrong conclusion from their observations and need to be set straight.

Making Working Committees Work

Where a community committee most needs professional help is in defining the range of possibilities open to it. It is unreasonable to ask such a group to formulate what it wants out of thin air, with no grasp of possible alternatives. It is necessary to be very clear about the relative realism of various courses of action. If the whole planning exercise is simply devoted to showing what ought to happen in the future, without any definite appropriation of funds in sight, it is important that everyone understands that at once—and don't be surprised if interest immediately evaporates. Except in cases where the municipal authorities are hopelessly intransigent, this kind of "shopping list" planning does not serve a very useful purpose. Community groups will accept realistic limitations, even when they don't approve of them.

Once a working group does make some decisions, it is also helpful if it sticks to them. I remember taking a working committee for a historic restoration through an impeccably Rogersian series of decisions, only to have the head of the group challenge a basic concept at a very late stage when designs (tactics) were almost complete. I pointed out that the whole approach had been devised in order to accommodate a concept that he himself had put forward, and read him the chapter and verse in the minutes of the working committee. "Well, I was wrong before," he replied, completely unrepentant.

Advantages of Community Participation

Despite all the pitfalls, any form of community consultation and participation is clearly superior to the alternative method of planning by confrontation. It can be argued that community participation is automatically required by modern neighborhood development plans that substitute selective renewal and rehabilitation for old-style "urban removal." If you intend to knock down a neighborhood, there may not be much point in working with the local community, which is not likely to react favorably. But if some or all of the people in the area are to remain, the planning process almost has to include them.

Community participation does not eliminate painful choices, yet people are more willing to make such decisions when they understand the reasons for them; and an open process in which all decisions are explained helps defuse suspicion.

If planners and designers ask the right questions, a few meetings with community groups can also tell them as much about the residents as a sociological survey, without insulting the residents and making them feel they are regarded as guinea pigs, which, unfortunately, is the effect of most surveys. Community meetings are also a good way to assess local priorities. Garbage collection and the number of welfare families being placed in the area may be much hotter issues than housing conditions.

Planners and designers should not expect much in the way of specific positive suggestions from community meetings; it is necessary to make specific proposals to the community. These will get plenty of reaction. When people see the changes they suggested showing up on the drawings at the next meeting, they will begin to believe that they really are participating in drawing up the plans.

Of course, there are always going to be some issues where the community's views cannot be decisive. A locality's reaction to a proposed expressway is more likely to be "We don't need it" than "Let us help you plan the best route." And don't expect a community to accept "the greatest good of the greatest number" when it goes dead against its own interest.

Community participation also has its undeniably messy aspects. It is hard to keep people from coming to meetings and using the proceedings as their therapy group; intransigent people with particular agendas in mind may try to hold a project hostage, no matter what reasonable attempts are made to accommodate them.

One could go a long way toward eliminating the imperfections in the community participation process by creating decentralized local government in larger cities. If communities could make local planning and design decisions through established institutions of neighborhood government, rather than through ad hoc consultative committees, the whole process would be more stable and more effective, and would come much closer to the town meeting ideal.

In big cities, decentralized planning still leaves the need for some kind of integrative planning mechanism to deal with large-scale issues like highways. London has been experimenting for years with the devolution of local planning decisions without eliminating controversy and complaints from communities. However, community participation is here to stay. On balance, it is a major improvement in the way urban design and planning decisions are made.

How long does it take to get some little red stop signs on that alley? We have been talking about that for six months and all we get out of those bureaucrats is bullshit.

How long is this temporary closing going to be? We never saw no questionnaire out of City Hall. They never asked me a thing.

If you look back in that big brick garage you'll see the owner's Rolls-Royce. Somebody must be doing OK in this neighborhood.

Whatever they write about this neighborhood better be good or else we'll stop that whole publication. We want positive things in print about us.

You wouldn't believe the things people will say at a public hearing but I was there, and that's what they said.

That little carriage house back there on the corner would take $38,000 to fix it up and you can buy one of these whole houses for that money. Who's going to fix it up with figures like that there?

When we moved in here it was just all run down, and now there's a bunch of us owners, fixing up. But it's getting to be a battleground, with all that commerce coming down on us.

THE CHANGING CONTEXT FOR URBAN DESIGN

4

Urban Design and the Preservation Movement

The historic preservation movement is the most important change to have occurred to architecture and urban design since the so-called Modern movement, which can be considered its antithesis. The "modern" movement in architecture looked with disdain upon buildings of the nineteenth and twentieth centuries that were adorned with the trappings of earlier historical periods. Such "eclectic" buildings were outside the "mainstream" of architectural history, and so could be disregarded.

Historic preservation can be called a form of architectural criticism because it grew stronger on the outrage created when beloved buildings were torn down and replaced by structures that people liked a good deal less.

I participated, with many other architects, in the singularly futile gesture of forming a picket line in front of New York City's Pennsylvania Station in August 1962 to protest the impending demolition of this most civilized evocation of the classical past, with a train shed that even historians of "modern" architecture thought was important. Needless to add, the demonstration did not stop the building being replaced by an office building and a sports arena.

A few months later, the architect Max Abramovitz told an audience at the Architectural League of New York that he could not understand the sentiment for saving Pennsylvania Station. When he was a young man, he added, he would have been picketing to have it torn down.

I doubt if Max Abramovitz or any other leading architect would make such a statement today. Somewhere in the early 1970s the pendulum swung in the other direction; historic preservation and the adaptive re-use of old buildings have become a stronger and stronger political force.

The point has been reached where many people seem to feel that any new building will be worth less than any old building. Preservation as a form of hostility to modernism has in turn helped promote a reexamination of the basic concepts of modern architecture. Under the slogan of "post-modernism," architects have begun to explore the ornament and elaboration that had been rejected in the name of efficiency and machine production. Now the work of once-despised "eclectics" is being reevaluated with a greater understanding of what these architects were trying to do.

The effect of preservation on urban design has been no less strong. No longer do people talk about improvements that require the clearing of whole districts of a city. More and more, urban renewal and redevelopment take the form of a mixture of old and new, for both economic and aesthetic reasons. Today we must be on guard against being too strong an advocate of historic preservation, a question we will come back to later in this chapter.

Some buildings are more worth preserving than others, or at least are worth preserving for different reasons. For discussion, we can arrange our consideration of preservation and adaptive re-use along a spectrum of vulnerability to change. At one end of the spectrum we have buildings of overwhelming architectural or historical importance, whose preservation these days is beyond question, although they may have been threatened in the past: Mt. Vernon; Richardson's Allegheny County Courthouse in Pittsburgh; Maybeck's First Church of Christ, Scientist in Berkeley, California. Buildings in this category are preserved as museums or remain in their original use, appreciated and well cared for by their owners.

Unfortunately, there are many structures of great historical or artistic merit that are not important enough to be made into museums and that no longer have an economic use, or whose site is potentially the location for a more lucrative real estate investment. Zoning laws, and the principle of uniform administration, have traditionally made no distinctions about the nature of buildings in a zoning district. A building with a floor-area ratio of 3, in a district that permits 18, is more valuable dead than alive if there is a strong real estate market, no matter how important its architecture or associations may be.

The way to preserve such buildings involves a combination of landmarks designation, new federal tax incentives, ingenious adaptive re-use, plus a dose of good old-fashioned yelling and screaming by preservation advocates.

Then there is the historic district, whose individual buildings may not be of landmark quality, but whose overall character is significant. The recognition of the historic district principle represents an enlargement of the concept of preservation. A new tall building, even if it goes up on an empty lot, may violate the integrity of such a district.

At the far end of the spectrum are buildings that are merely old, but whose useful life could be prolonged. In the past, such buildings were usually considered incumbrances that stood in the way of the highest and best use of properties. Today, they are more valuable, partly because of our new acceptance of old buildings, partly because of construction economics. It is with this kind of building that we are beginning to see examples of the political pendulum having swung too far. Environmental Impact Statements and other planning procedures often require that experts examine buildings to assess their historic and architectural value. And here is the problem: Is there an expert who is prepared to say that a particular structure is totally without merit? Well, let us leave the question of excessive historic preservation, for the time being, and take our issues in order: land-marks designation, tax incentives for preservation, historic districts, adaptive re-use, and old buildings in general.

The story of the proposed office tower using the air rights over Grand Central Station in New York City illustrates how landmark designation can be used to help preserve a significant building. The litigation in this case produced an important U.S. Supreme Court decision, with implications for preservation all over the country.

Grand Central Terminal was designed as a monument to Commodore Vanderbilt in a lavish and palatial style evocative of both ancient Rome and Napoleonic France. Its classical dress is done with great originality, however, and its functional organization as a terminal is brilliant. For decades it has been a landmark in the true sense of the word, known around the world as one of New York City's major gateways.

It was designated a landmark in 1967, soon after the New York City Landmarks Commission came into existence. At that time the Landmarks Law protected only exteriors; since then it has been amended to permit the designation of interior landmarks and the interior of Grand Central's main concourse has also been designated. Designation of facades or interiors is still only a procedure for delaying demolition two years, if an owner is determined to take down the building.

In the late sixties, the Penn-Central Railroad decided to develop the air rights of the Terminal by placing a large office tower over the existing building. The zoning permits a floor-area ratio of 15, or 18 with a plaza, and the floor area of the terminal, despite its substantial bulk, is only 1.5. No plaza was possible, but an office building with an area of 13.5 times the 4-acre site was permitted by the zoning—a very large building indeed.

The late Marcel Breuer accepted the commission to design the office tower over the Terminal. An internationally known architect and a former faculty member at the Bauhaus, Breuer saw nothing incongruous in what was proposed, except that it seemed to him un-

THE CHANGING CONTEXT FOR URBAN DESIGN

necessary to go to so much trouble to preserve the Terminal facades, which, in his eyes, were a provincial version of a decadent French classicism.

The Landmarks Commission, however, took the position that a 700-foot-high office building over the Terminal constituted an alteration to the facade, and they refused to approve the new building.

One of the legal questions raised by this decision is whether the Landmarks Commission, by its ruling, is depriving the owners of the building of the right to do anything at all with their property. If that should be the case, the city has, in effect, condemned it, and should pay the owner compensation. The city would be incapable of paying the enormous sum necessary, as landmarks preservation cannot be given priority over new schools and hospitals, except, oddly enough, in Russia and the socialist countries of Eastern Europe.

Knowing that this issue would come up, the Planning Commission devised a way to give the owners of landmarks a third alternative to the choice between demolition and the status quo. It passed a law permitting the transfer of "air rights" from a landmark to nearby properties.

The result is that the owner of a neighboring piece of land can purchase some of the unused bulk permitted by the zoning on the landmark property. The overall density of the zoning district remains the same, and the owners of the landmark can participate in some of the advantages of new development.

This law was particularly applicable in the case of Grand Central Terminal as the Penn-Central Railroad owned a large number of adjacent properties. The whole Terminal area from 42nd to 50th Streets on both sides of Park Avenue had originally been developed over railroad yards, to a master development plan of architectural and urbanistic distinction. Since the 1950s the Penn-Central had been redeveloping its properties, one building at a time, without any attempt to exploit the possibilities that such a large property holding suggests.

Using the air rights from the Terminal would cause

One of the proposals by Marcel Breuer for a building over Grand Central Terminal. This version would have removed much of the principle facade and obscured the rest.

the Penn-Central to give some thought to a staged master redevelopment plan, something they should have done years before.

The City Planning Commission's Urban Design Group prepared some alternate studies showing the difference between the Penn-Central plan and various possibilities created by the air rights transfer. These schemes were particularly persuasive at the Landmarks Commission's public hearing in pointing out the physical effect of the Breuer scheme on future development in the area: the destruction of an invaluable "air park" over the station itself—a major breathing space for midtown and for the railroad's own properties, which surrounded the Terminal. The Urban Design Group schemes would save the air park by transferring the development rights to a number of nearby sites also owned by the Penn-Central, so that the twenty- to thirty-year development picture would be much the same as it is today: a low and handsome landmark surrounded by a ring of new high buildings. The result would be to preserve a fine building and improve the future design of a large part of midtown Manhattan.

The Penn-Central and the developer agreed to build under the new legislation. They went ahead with specific plans for an office block (also by Breuer) and a small park, both on the site of the Biltmore Hotel. This development utilized a substantial amount of the available transfer rights while "banking" the rest for future use. One reason the air rights transfer legislation was passed was that the city had come to believe that the developer would build under its provisions. However, over the next six months the office market changed; the developer was caught in a situation where he could neither afford to build nor get out of his contract with Penn-Central, which was just declaring bankruptcy. Within a year both parties had decided that it was in their own best interest to file suit against the city's new Landmarks Law as depriving them of their development rights.

A Landmark Legal Decision

After years of litigation, the Supreme Court of the United States determined in 1978 that the New York City Landmarks Preservation Law did not have the

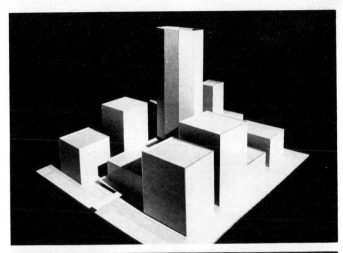

The top block model shows the area around Grand Central Terminal as it is; Center: as it would have been if the Breuer proposal had been built and other nearby blocks also redeveloped; the third model, bottom, shows the Urban Design Group proposal to use the air rights to redevelop two sites to the west, also shown in the site plan below right.

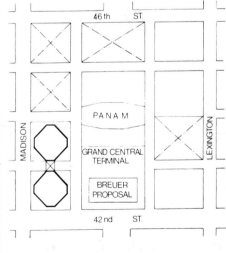

effect of condemning private property for public use without compensation, and that the law was comprehensive in its approach to landmark structures even if it resulted in the designation of scattered pieces of property. The Court thus did not get to the question of whether the transfer of development rights would constitute appropriate compensation for a "taking" of property, although it noted the mitigating effect of development rights transfer on the economic problems created by landmark designation.

Some of these Grand Central Terminal development rights have subsequently been sold to the Philip Morris Building development across the street, showing that air rights transfer was not merely a theoretical possibility.

Because the original plans for Grand Central included a tower that was never built, it is possible that this story is not yet over. The Landmarks Preservation Commission would have a hard time certifying that the original architects' own proposal for a tower was architecturally inappropriate; and there are rumors of a plan to build a replica (at least as far as externals are concerned) of Warren & Wetmore's original design. Rumor also has it that some of the stonework might be carried out in a plastic, to reduce weight and make the structure more economical.

Tax Incentives for Preservation

Since the Federal Tax Reform Act of 1976 there have been tax incentives for preserving old buildings and disincentives against tearing them down.

The latest regulations, enacted in 1981, use an investment tax credit as the basic incentive, replacing depreciation incentives which were made less significant by a general revision of depreciation schedules. The 1981 act also extended tax benefits to all older buildings, officially historic or not.

The tax credit is 15 percent for buildings between thirty and forty years old, 20 percent for older buildings, and 25 percent for historic structures, provided that the investment is for "substantial" rehabilitation. Historic structures are those on the National Register of Historic Places, or significant structures within historic districts that are on the National Register, or in

THE CHANGING CONTEXT FOR URBAN DESIGN

locally designated districts where the legal procedures for designation are essentially similar to the National Register process and the local law is approved by the U.S. Department of the Interior. Curiously enough, locally designated individual landmark buildings are not eligible for tax benefits, although such buildings are often eligible for inclusion on the National Register.

The rehabilitation plans are certified through application to the state historic preservation officer and then by review at the Department of the Interior.

An owner can depreciate the full value of the investment in a historic structure, but must deduct the value of the tax credit in computing depreciation for older buildings that are not deemed historic.

If an owner demolishes a building on the National Register, or a structure within a registered historic district that has not been "decertified" by the Interior Department, the costs of demolition will be treated as a land cost for tax purposes (i.e., no depreciation).

Clarifications in the 1981 law make it easier to give away easements that divest historic buildings of unwanted development rights.

These recent tax laws give a new status to the concept of a historic district. We are familiar with the idea that New Orleans's Vieux Carré or Boston's Beacon Hill are historic districts; but an old factory and surrounding blocks of workers housing may also qualify. When you get into district designation, you are no longer talking just about buildings but about the economic and social life of a whole quarter of a city. Indeed, the ambiance itself is often what ought to be preserved.

The historic district concept is related to the back-to-the-city movement, which has also had such a strong effect on community participation in planning (see Chapter 3). The children whose parents had moved them to the suburbs so that they could have every advantage are moving back to the city to have a more convenient location and spacious old houses with interesting character and details. The movement is also economic; these older houses are often a much better value than their suburban counterparts as far as space and building construction are concerned. Preservation is

Historic Districts

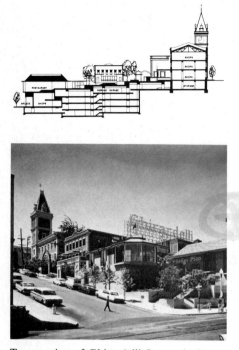

Top: section of Ghirardelli Square in San Francisco, showing how an old factory was adaptively re-used and new buildings added to make a modern specialty retailing center. Bottom: the view up Larkin Street shows the relationship of new buildings to old. Opposite: looking across Ghirardelli Square to San Francisco Bay, Alcatraz Island can be seen dimly in the background. The architects were Wurster, Bernardi & Emmons, the site planner and landscape architect, Lawrence Halprin.

Adaptive Re-Use

important, too; many of these families enjoy fixing up an older house that has been neglected. Sometimes the back-to-the-city movement is referred to as "gentrification," a wry term that originated in England and refers to the class difference between the people who are buying these old houses and the people who were living there before and have to move. When a neighborhood becomes "gentrified," prices rise for the older group of residents still living in unrestored houses. If there is a historic district designation, it may enforce a standard of appearance that is unsympathetic to the taste of these earlier settlers, or simply beyond their means.

There are now some government programs that are designed to keep life in a historic district within the means of lower-income people with previous ties to the area. Those in use in the Manchester district of Pittsburgh are a good example. Among the tools available are low-interest loans made possible when the city borrows in the municipal loan market and passes the interest savings on to homeowners, and facade easements, where the city takes title to the exterior of the building and then invests in the capital costs of rehabilitation—normally with federal community development funds. The city also makes condemned, tax-delinquent properties available to new owners at nominal cost, provided the new owners fix them up to a level that meets city requirements.

Such measures can mitigate the adverse effects of social change in historic districts; however, the dynamics of real estate in a private market always mean that someone profits at someone else's expense. On balance, the preservation and restoration of old neighborhoods has to be considered valuable for the economic health of a city, even if there is hardship for individuals.

The new tax incentives encourage adaptive re-use; it is not necessary to preserve the original purpose of the structure in order to qualify for favorable tax treatment. There are other incentives for adaptive re-use besides the tax laws. Inflation has given existing structures an economic value that they did not have before in our disposal-oriented economy. Even now, it is not axiomatic that saving an existing structure saves money, as

THE CHANGING CONTEXT FOR URBAN DESIGN

The Quincy Market in Boston when it was still a wholesale market, the original architect being Matthew Parish. Many of the buildings had been altered over time.

the eccentricities and complications of existing structures can raise costs. However, the possibility of reusing existing buildings has become worth considering, which is a fundamental change in the real estate market.

The architectural character of old buildings has also acquired a positive value, particularly for downtown specialty retailing. Ghirardelli Square in San Francisco, completed in 1964, was one of the first projects to make a marketing plus out of buildings that had—up to that time—been treated as drab and outmoded.

Ghirardelli Square also set a pattern by recreating a past that, if you enquired closely, had never actually existed. A routine industrial building with a few interesting architectural touches was transformed into a fantasy land of terraces and gazebos, and thus became an ideal home for a new kind of specialty shopping center.

Now almost every city has its analogue to Ghirardelli

Square: Pioneer Square in Seattle, Trolley Square in Salt Lake City, Bakery Square in Louisville, Station Square in Pittsburgh, and most impressive of all, the Faneuil Hall Market in Boston.

The Faneuil Hall Market is probably the best known of these urban specialty centers built after Ghirardelli Square. It has provided much-needed diversity and reinforcement to the land-use pattern in downtown Boston; it is a tourist and entertainment attraction; as the photographs above show, it has rescued a series of fine old buildings that had been mistreated and whose old use was fading. It is a financial success for the developer, James Rouse & Co., and for the Boston Redevelopment Authority; and it has brought well-deserved awards to the architects, Benjamin Thompson & Associates.

When the Faneuil Hall Market is such a textbook example of urban revitalization, it may seem churlish to

The Quincy Market with original rooflines restored and the complex remodeled as part of the Faneuil Hall specialty retailing complex. The architects were Benjamin Thompson & Associates. Below: a detail of the market, showing what a successful new urban element the area has become.

say anything bad about it. However, while it is a successful adaptive re-use, it is not necessarily a happy example of historic preservation. In order to turn the old market into a modern retailing and food service environment, Thompson's design and the Rouse Company management have changed the character of the buildings, bringing to mind the transformation of Lady Montdore in Nancy Mitford's novel *Love in a Cold Climate:*

Facial operations, slimming cures, exercises, massage, diet, make-up, new clothes, jewels reset, a blue rinse for her gray hair, pink bows and diamond daisies in the blue curls. . . . In my opinion it was not successful, for she made the sacrifice of a grand and characteristic appearance without really gaining in prettiness. . . .

Interior of the rotunda in the central market building at Quincy Market.

THE CHANGING CONTEXT FOR URBAN DESIGN

The question of fidelity to a building's original character is only at issue when buildings of real architectural distinction or historic importance are preserved through adaptive re-use. However, there are a great many old railway stations, central post offices, and schools that were some of the best buildings of their day but are no longer needed for their original purpose. Their future probably depends on ingenious adaptive re-use, but how it is done is an issue; these buildings should be allowed to grow old gracefully.

It may be that adaptive re-use and preservation that are faithful to the architect's original intent may require some sacrifice of financial return, which in turn points up the need for a new kind of real estate developer, whose primary purpose is preservation rather than the maximum figure on the "bottom line" of the financial statement.

The concept of a not-for-profit or limited-profit entrepreneur may seem paradoxical, but we are starting to see such people emerge. They use the methods of the

Above left: the interior of the Pittsburgh and Lake Erie Railway Station in Pittsburgh before it was remodeled, as shown above right, into a restaurant that is part of the Station Square complex. The biggest change was that the skylight, which had been covered over, was restored; but the room today is, in a quiet way, more opulently Edwardian than it ever was originally.

Detail of the shops built in the old Freight House at Station Square in Pittsburgh.

The Not-for-Profit Entrepreneur

real estate developer, but their bottom line is architecture and preservation. Arthur Ziegler, the director of Pittsburgh's History and Landmarks Foundation, has created a good example of this method with the Station Square project. His organization has converted the main floor of the old Pittsburgh and Lake Erie Railway Station into an enormously successful restaurant. The rooms are discreetly more opulent and Edwardian than they appear in old photographs, but the old, slightly gritty flavor of the railway station is maintained. Adjacent to the station is the Freight House, a restaurant and specialty shopping center in the Ghirardelli Square tradition; but the original structure was a simple shed, so that a little hokeyness is both acceptable and necessary.

Unfortunately, the hotel at Station Square deviates from the original, highly sophisticated site plan, which had been drawn by Urban Design Associates, and ends up not doing justice to either its historic setting or its prominent site. The not-for-profit entrepreneur needs to find ways of making sure that partners don't simply carry on business as usual.

While Station Square has a higher equity investment (something like $7 million from the Scaife Foundation), and was far more risky than conventional real estate projects, it is beginning to look as if it may be a profitable operation. If so, the profits will be used to subsidize other History and Landmarks Foundation operations where the chances for commercial profit do not exist.

The Preservation Ethic

Finally, we come to the question of preserving older buildings in general, whether or not they have architectural or historic merit, whether or not there are immediate economic or sales advantages in preserving them. In a period in which we are aware that our resources are limited, and have begun to see the consequences of scarcity, preservation has become an ethical question. As stated eloquently by Dwight Rettie of the National Park Service,* we must cultivate a conservation ethic, not only for our own immediate advantage but because we are custodians of the world's resources for future generations. Old buildings have a value, just because

*Dwight Rettie, in a foreword to *Children and the Urban Environment: a Learning Experience* by Marshall Kaplan, et al. New York: Praeger, 1972.

they are there; and replacing them means using more energy and natural resources than conserving them.

Having said all this, there may still be occasions when it makes sense to tear down an old building, particularly if preservation gets in the way of a major new project that itself has many positive features. Improving cities is a complex business at best, and it is much easier to stop projects than it is to put them together. We are beginning to see what could be called a preservation neurosis, which constructs a rationale for preserving everything. When I was working on the master plan for the Gateway National Recreation Area in New York City, the historians for the National Park Service were with difficulty dissuaded from putting the parking lot at Riis Park on the National Register of Historic Places. The reason: At the time it was built, it was rumored to be the largest parking lot in the world. The plan for the Riis Park portion of Gateway shows that, in the future, this 9,000-car parking lot should be broken up into several smaller, landscaped units. Admittedly an extreme example, but surely the advantages in improving the experience of arrival at Riis Park outweigh the alleged loss of historic character.

Everything that is old is not necessarily better than anything that is new, no matter how tempted we may sometimes be to think so. As the preservation movement has increased in sophistication, there has been wide acceptance of the concept that sometimes it is necessary to make an informed choice among competing claims. A sense of proportion is necessary in preservation, as in most other activities.

We can be sure that the preservation movement has permanently changed both urban design and architecture. We are more concerned with making use of what we already have, we are more sensitive to architectural context and continuity, and we have learned that you can't make the whole world over every few years. Urban design will be more concerned with incremental units, with flexibility; and architecture will be more concerned with experience, relationships, and remembrance of things past.

The Preservation Neurosis

Discussion

PART TWO

DESIGNING CITIES WITHOUT DESIGNING BUILDINGS

5

Zoning, Mapping, and Urban Renewal as Urban Design Techniques

Most of our cities and suburbs have been constructed by private investors. While the government builds or participates in the financing of an increasing number of structures, it seems likely that the majority of the buildings we see around us will continue to be initiated by private enterprise for a long time to come.

Real estate developers have one overwhelmingly obvious objective: they want to make money; and, as they are in a high-risk business, they want to make a great deal of money. Some people who are concerned about the future of the environment feel that it is wrong that the guiding principle of development should be the profit motive, and even the real estate investor is likely to agree that private enterprise has generally not been successful in creating satisfactory cities, or in conserving the natural landscape.

To understand the limitations of real estate development, you should think of it as proceeding according to a set of rules essentially similar to those governing the game of Monopoly. You probably remember that the Monopoly board is marked off into squares, most of which are named after places in Atlantic City, New Jersey: Oriental Avenue, Marvin Gardens, Boardwalk. Players throw dice to move around the board. If you land on a street that no other player owns (and you have enough money), you can buy it. When you have assembled all the streets in the same color group, you can improve them with "houses" and "hotels," charging more and more exploitive rents to other players who land on your property.

The surveyor has marked off most of our cities and towns into a real-life Monopoly board of lots; and even in the most rural areas, the invisible but unyielding lines of property have been superimposed on the natural landscape.

When you look down on a landscape from an airplane, the underlying game board is revealed most clearly. Here stands a new, raw street with houses under construction; next door is an old-fashioned estate with its lawns and woods intact; then more new houses, next a farm still in cultivation, a highway interchange with a small shopping center and a motel nearby, then more houses, and another farm, and so on. The pursuit of profit is what shapes our environment.

The developer of the houses or the shopping center, like the Monopoly player, has first to assemble enough lots that have not been "improved" to their full economic potential so that there is room for a new development. Assemblage must take place as secretly as possible, because, if other players of the real estate game find out what the developer is up to, they might move to block the assemblage; or the owners of the properties could hold out for a higher price.

Often, the location of a new development is determined by ease of assemblage as much as by more logical land-use factors. An old lady's attachment to the estate her father built, or a young farmer's determination to stick to the land in the face of tempting offers and rising property taxes, deflect the entrepreneur to other properties more easily developed. The result is the familiar urban sprawl, where the old pattern is lost but no satisfactory new pattern is created.

If your aim were to create a situation in which cities were developed in a coherent fashion, you would not use the game of "real estate" as it is now played. Nothing is more damaging to coherence and planning than the creation of a large number of arbitrarily shaped lots, with their ownership divided among thousands of individuals.

DESIGNING CITIES WITHOUT DESIGNING BUILDINGS

Similarly, if you wished to conserve the natural land-scape, and give new settlements a compact and coherent form, you would not mark the land off along arbitrary geometric lines and let use and function fall where they may.

The secrecy required for land assemblage is another factor that makes coherence and planning difficult to achieve, and the competitive nature of the game creates unnecessary duplication, fragmenting the urban pattern even more.

There are established alternatives to land development based on profit. For example, the city of Stockholm purchased most of the land surrounding it in the early part of this century, and has thus been able to exercise total control over its development and growth. Great Britain, in the Town and Country Planning Act of 1947, moved, in effect, to nationalize the land, as have the socialist countries of Eastern Europe.

While private development has its limitations, development through government control is also far from perfect. If private real estate entrepreneurs produce too fragmentary and wasteful a result, development controlled by governmental agencies can be slow and cumbersome, and its product unimaginative and stereotyped. The bureaucratic system does not seem as successful as the marketplace in providing for a wide range of human desires and experiences.

In any event, large-scale government spending for land acquisition, or as compensation for land nationalization, doesn't seem likely to happen in the United States in the immediate future. In the meantime, the game of real estate goes on, and some method needs to be found to direct and improve it.

The next time you see an announcement of a new town, or a major urban redevelopment project, you should examine the drawing published in the newspaper and ask yourself what will happen to the design concept when, as is usual, portions of the project are parceled out to different developers and architects over a period of ten to thirty years. The forces at work on our cities are so diverse, and the rate of social change has accelerated so rapidly, that it is most unlikely that such a large project—if it is constructed at all—will end up looking much like the original design. All too often, the merit of the published design derives from the architecture of the proposed buildings rather than from any underlying coherence in the plan itself. What if the buildings are not all the same height or are not placed at precisely the angle shown in the drawings? What if materials vary; what if changes in architectural taste occur? What if changes in function or economics force major changes in size or shape of buildings? Will the design still make sense?

Another, more difficult question: What about those parts of our cities and towns where large-scale redevelopment will not occur, only a process of piecemeal modifications on a block-by-block, or even lot-by-lot, basis? Is there any way to plan such areas so that they come to have the coherence of a group of buildings designed at one time? Is there an alternative to architectural consistency that will still produce a unified design for a new town or a major development?

There is a planning process that could achieve just such a purpose and that is already in use every day, but it has been the province of the lawyer, the surveyor, and the municipal engineer. They have considered their primary task to be, not control over design but over more abstract considerations of public health and welfare. Unintentionally, however, the lawyer, the surveyor, and the engineer have determined the basic design framework of the American city, through a combination of local zoning regulations and the street pattern, neither of which has been enacted with its design implications in mind.

Zoning is a forbiddingly technical subject that even lawyers have a tendency to avoid if they can, while street mapping is considered a routine matter of little conceptual interest. As you learn more about these little-known technical specialties, however, you realize that they provide important clues to the solution of the fundamental problem of city design: How can you design a city if you can't design all the buildings?

Zoning, as its names implies, is a process of dividing a city up into zones, each of which has different legal requirements. Within each zone, regulations specify the size and shape of the building that can be placed on the land, and the uses to which buildings can be put.

The first American zoning ordinance was enacted in New York City in 1916, with the aim of imposing some minimum standards of light and air for streets, which, particularly in lower Manhattan, had become increasingly dark and canyon-like as buildings grew taller and taller. It also sought to separate activities that were viewed as incompatible, such as the factories of the garment center and the fashionable shops and homes along Fifth Avenue.

The regulations specified what activities could take place in each zone, and imposed "setbacks" on buildings above a certain height to permit sunlight to fall on the streets and sidewalks, and light and air to reach the interiors of the buildings. There were also some absolute restrictions on the size of buildings in certain zones, in order to make the central areas the most intensively used districts.

City planning courses teach that zoning regulations represent the means for implementing master plans; but the first New York City zoning resolution predates the establishment of the New York City Planning Commission by twenty-two years, and the publication of the city's first comprehensive plan by fifty-three years. The experience of other American cities has been similar, showing that zoning first, planning afterwards, is the usual sequence.

While zoning regulations are far from being a master plan, it is easy to forget, now that their use has become routine, what an enormous restriction of property rights the enactment of zoning represented. Owners of land were used to the idea that, if they owned a piece of property, they could do what they wished with it—subject at most to some deed restrictions. The legal rationale for zoning is the so-called police power of the states to make regulations to protect public health, safety, and general welfare. The principle of the police power as a means to regulate land use was affirmed by the Supreme Court decision upholding the zoning law adopted by Euclid, Ohio, in 1922.

TENEMENT HOUSE ACT. 1800's — COMP. PLAN. 1916.

EUCLID VS AMBER REALTY 1926

Studies by Hugh Ferriss showing building masses are "carved" out of the zoning setback lines of New York City's 1916 ordinance.

Opposite: the Fifth Avenue frontage of Central Park shows how the zoning setback lines have determined the design of the buildings.

Prior to "Euclid," the consensus of the legal profession had been that such regulations as a uniform setback line required condemnation of the land by the municipality. This was the opinion set down in the famous 1909 plan for Chicago, based on the designs of Daniel Burnham, in which Burnham sought to apply to this most American of cities the avenues, rond-points, and palatial architecture that Baron Haussmann had used to re-plan Paris during the Second Empire.

Many elements of the Burnham plan that could be carried out directly by the city, such as the park system, the extension of Michigan Avenue, and major public buildings, have been realized. Where the Chicago plan failed was in the regulation of private development, because, in 1909, the only legal way to exercise such control was for the municipality to buy up the land and buildings.

For years, no one made the connection between the design objectives of plans like Chicago's and "Euclid," with its controls based on health and safety. Architects and designers who knew all about Burnham's plan had no concept of the design implications of zoning.

But zoning, whatever its rationale and intention, is as strong a design control as any element in the Burnham plan. The setbacks created by New York's 1916 zoning changed the tall building from the straight towers of the early skyscrapers to the pyramidal masses illustrated by Hugh Ferriss in the drawings on this page. The photograph of the Fifth Avenue frontage of Central Park opposite shows how zoning determined the design of a whole avenue as surely as the vision of the autocratic Baron Haussmann shaped the boulevards of Paris.

A parallel situation exists in the case of street mapping, where governments lay out streets which also have extensive design implications that were largely unintended or based upon antiquated and stereotyped ideas. As a result, the engineer and the surveyor have had a far greater influence over the design and planning of our cities than the architect or the city planner. Until very recently, city governments were only expected to provide essential services; except among some professionals, city planning was looked upon as a form of

DESIGNING CITIES WITHOUT DESIGNING BUILDINGS

"If a city can get the buildings it asks for, why can't it get the buildings it wants?"

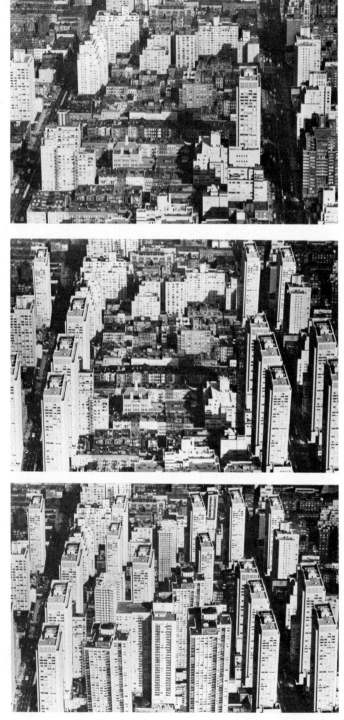

A Manhattan block as it is today . . .

. . . as it would look if it were fully developed in accordance with the zoning

. . . . . . finally, what would happen if the highest-density zoning were extended to the middle of the block, as many developers wish.

DESIGNING CITIES WITHOUT DESIGNING BUILDINGS

municipal engineering, a governmental service like clean streets and city water. Planners were careful to keep their regulations within the traditional requirements of zoning, such as the preservation of light and air, or to ask for no more than was needed to supply appropriate drainage gradients and other engineering criteria. Great care was taken to seem as objective as possible, and anything that might appear in the least arbitrary or subjective was rigorously excluded from public policy.

The reason that grids of streets, all intersecting at right angles, have inexorably covered so much of our landscape is that they were viewed as rational and objective. The gridiron plan produces large numbers of lots of similar size that can readily be located on a map and meet various bureaucratic requirements for access, utility lines, and so on.

While it is easy to blame greedy real estate developers for row after row of "ticky-tacky" look-alike houses, in many cases the combination of street grid and zoning setback lines has left the builder no alternative. If you find the skyline of the average American city to be full of unimaginative boxy buildings, the combination of zoning rules and street grid must, again, bear at least part of the blame.

As you learn more about zoning and mapping, you see that, very often, the design of a new building is virtually specified by the regulations. Few new structures are unaffected by some sort of governmental control. We are left with the question: If a city can get the buildings it asks for, why can't it get the buildings it needs and wants?

City planners and other responsible officials can no longer take refuge in a cult of objectivity and impersonality, because a decision-making process that does not consider the consequences of an action does not relieve the government of responsibility for the results. Government controls over development have become pervasive. Now they need to become positive in nature, a specification of what should be done rather than a prohibition of what should not.

Zoning laws have been for real estate what the Mar-

Another illustration of the way zoning requirements shape design. The black area is the only permissible place on the lot for the building.

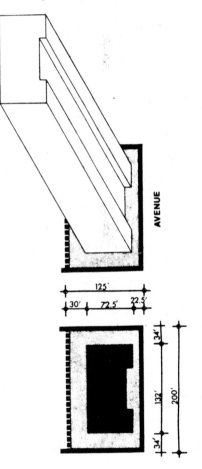

quis of Queensberry rules were to boxing. They set up rules of conduct and define what constitutes a "low blow" against the public interest: houses set too close together, office buildings that block each other's light and air, a noisy factory being introduced into a quiet residential area. Because zoning has rarely been a positive force, in the sense of shaping the built environment to a predetermined pattern, zoning regulations have tended to pull development inward, away from property boundaries, on the theory that the public interest most in need of protection is represented by the rights of adjoining property owners. Such setback and bulk controls take no account of topography, orientation, or the nature of existing buildings in the area; nor does the land-use separation enforced by zoning generally take into account the possibilities created by modern construction, air conditioning, and artificial illumination.

In the case of highly complex urban centers like midtown and lower Manhattan, the public interest may be much better served by the interconnection of buildings and the mixture of complementary land uses, just as, in suburban areas, the public may be better served by clusters of houses and neighborhood shopping, rather than the even distribution of single-family houses over the entire landscape, and a shopping center out by the Interstate.

If conventional zoning controls have so many defects, why not get rid of them altogether? After all, Houston, Texas, has no zoning and it is not noticeably worse off than many another American city. And isn't zoning used as an instrument of exclusion to enforce residential segregation in suburbs? True enough, but Houston has an unusual development history that has permitted deed restrictions to perform many of the functions of zoning, and few people would argue seriously that our towns and cities would have been better off without land-use regulation, whatever its defects and the ways in which it has been misused. As Richard Babcock, one of the most articulate critics of zoning, has concluded: "There is little evidence in the history of land development in America that the private deci-

DESIGNING CITIES WITHOUT DESIGNING BUILDINGS

sion-maker, left to his own devices, can be trusted to act in the public interest."*

Perhaps the most important reason for keeping zoning controls, as well as mapping powers, is that they have been accepted by real estate entrepreneurs as part of the ordinary ground rules of development. The developer expects that there will be limitations on what can be done, so the cost of conforming to them is more or less discounted in the land price.

The existence of the controls thus represents a very valuable card in the hand of those seeking to improve the design and planning of towns and cities. If you can modify existing regulations to improve development without raising the cost to the developer, you have a far better chance of success than if you seek to impose new controls that have not been part of the rules up to now. New and more stringent regulations have a way of being defeated in the legislatures that must pass them; and new rules, designed to deal with a particular problem that has suddenly been brought to the attention of the authorities, can be struck down in the courts if they cannot be shown to have general application.

*Richard F. Babcock, *The Zoning Game: Municipal Practices and Policies.* Madison, Wis.: University of Wisconsin Press, 1966.

Three Kinds of Design Control:

The three most commonly used methods of overcoming the defects of traditional zoning regulations have been planned unit development, urban renewal controls, and zoning incentives.

1. Planned Unit Development

Planned unit development (PUD), sometimes known as cluster zoning, is used in rural and suburban areas that are being intensively developed for the first time. Ordinary zoning regulations can be suspended for a particular property. The developer, instead, submits a master plan that, within the same overall density, produces higher-density clusters of housing, leaving significant areas of the tract in their natural state. If the plan is approved, it becomes the development regulation for the property in question.

Planned unit development is also at least as much a street mapping technique as it is a zoning modification. In a PUD, only the major streets remain as ordinarily mapped; the subsidiary access and collector streets are

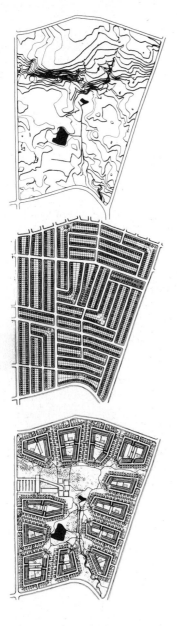

Three illustrations from New York City's Standards for Planned Unit Development, prepared by the Urban Design Group. Top: a tract of land in its natural state; center: the way the official city map and zoning requirements would shape development; and finally: the alternative possible under planned unit development.

planned at the same time as the buildings. The result is a street layout much more closely related to both the natural landscape and the design of the buildings than the "objective" gridiron plan and the lot-by-lot development it fosters.

The illustrations on pages 70 and 71 show two unusually accomplished examples of the kind of design required for planned unit development, both by a San Francisco architectural firm, Fisher-Friedman Associates.

Lighthouse Cove puts 124 townhouses on a 7.5-acre site in Redwood City, California. The property fronts on a natural lagoon and much of the internal public open space is an artificial body of water. Achieving high densities without loss of amenity is one important use for planned unit development.

Another important use is in situations where the terrain prevents conventional layouts. Turtle Rock Glen, within the Irvine planned community in California, puts fifty units of housing on two knolls that had been passed over in earlier planning.

The three drawings shown at left were made by New York City's Urban Design Group to illustrate what is permissible under planned unit development in New York City, where high-density zoning underlies most of the undeveloped areas within the city limits. A tract of land on Staten Island is shown as a contour map of its natural state, then covered by the gridiron of streets officially mapped for it, and finally as re-planned with loop streets and clustered houses that leave 35 percent of the land undisturbed.

The initial part of the Village Greens development, which was built on this land, follows a site plan very like the third drawing. A photograph of one of the housing clusters is shown on the opposite page.

An inner city example of the advantages of planned development can be seen when you compare two plans for the Crawford-Roberts Urban Renewal District in Pittsburgh. The first plan is entirely a product of the different zoning districts mapped for the area; the second, at the same density, permits a much more reasonable arrangement of houses.

Village Greens on Staten Island is a planned unit development built on some of the same tract of land shown on the opposite page. The architect is Norman Jaffe.

Two alternative site plans for the Crawford-Roberts Urban Renewal District in Pittsburgh. The top plan is what is required by the current zoning; the plan below is an alternative possible under planned development. Plan by John Valley of the Urban Redevelopment Authority of Pittsburgh, Jonathan Barnett, consultant.

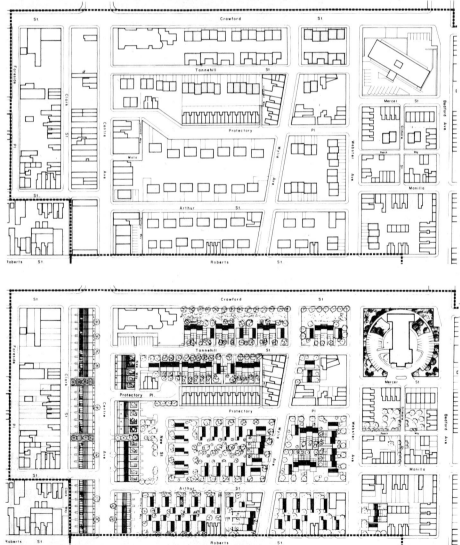

69

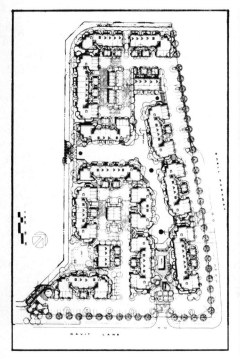

Above: site plan for Lighthouse Cove Planned Unit Development, Redwood Shores, California. Above right: a view of the internal lagoon looking toward the swim club.

2. Urban Renewal

Planned unit development is primarily a technique for new areas where you can wipe outmoded restrictions off the books and start with a clean slate and an undisturbed landscape. It is also applicable to urban renewal districts, as shown in the case of Crawford-Roberts; but urban renewal offers other, stronger means of regulating development.

Because of the insensitive way in which it has sometimes been used, urban renewal is known to its critics as "urban removal" or "the federal bulldozer." Cities have traditionally held the right of eminent domain, that is, the right to acquire private land by compulsory purchase for a public purpose. Over the years, the courts have extended the concept of public purpose until it has come to include many different forms of community improvements.

Under Title One of the Federal Housing Act of 1949, and its successors, the federal government used to provide funds to enable cities to obtain land by compulsory purchase, in areas that met certain criteria; then demolish the existing buildings; and sell the land at a loss

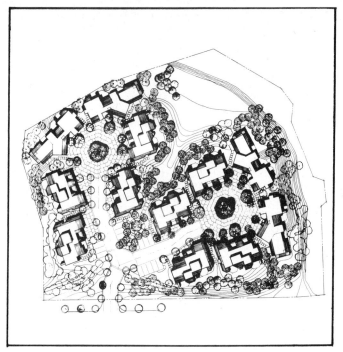

("write down") to developers who proposed to build something that the city considered desirable.

This technique, at least in theory, offers a high degree of design control, since the municipality, as the owner of the land, can set whatever conditions of sale it likes. In practice, urban renewal plans have seldom produced good city design, for lack of the design-control mechanisms that are described in the next chapter. The major criticisms of urban renewal have not been over design, however, but over the destructive effect of wholesale demolition of existing housing, stores, and industries on the lives of citizens and the economic health of the city. A better understanding of the complex interdependency of cities has led to a much more humane use of urban renewal powers only on selected sites rather than whole residential or commercial districts.

However, there are many instances when government-sponsored urban renewal in any form does not apply. This is particularly true of areas where property values are high, and which cannot be described as

Above left: site plan of Turtle Rock Glen, Irvine, California, showing how houses are clustered to preserve the natural terrain. Above: a view showing part of a house cluster. Both Lighthouse Cove and Turtle Rock Glen were designed by Fisher-Friedman Associates, of San Franciso.

3. Incentive Zoning

dilapidated, deteriorated, or otherwise appropriate for urban renewal. In such areas, zoning and mapping powers remain the best potential design control.

One such technique for controlling city design is the zoning incentive.

The comprehensive revision of New York City's zoning regulations made in 1961 was the first major attempt to use zoning incentives based in part on urban design considerations. Its most significant design feature was a provision that a developer could achieve an increase in floor area of up to 20 percent, in certain high-density commercial and residential districts, by providing a plaza that met the qualifications in the ordinance. Alternatively, a smaller bonus could be given for an arcade. San Francisco enacted zoning bonuses for arcades, plazas, and other amenities in 1966 (see page 126).

Letting developers build a larger building if they provide certain desirable features or amenities is a useful principle and a very valuable addition to the art of zoning regulation. It depends, of course, on the usual allowable limits being pitched to create smaller buildings than the market would otherwise permit. The bonus incentives in the New York law were introduced in partial compensation for a cut in the allowable size of buildings that in some cases amounted to as much as 50 percent. The passage of this zoning revision was a near miracle: one of the few cases where local real estate interests have agreed to a substantial decrease in zoned density. It became law because of the leadership and persuasive powers of the late James Felt, a real estate man himself, who was then the chairman of the New York City Planning Commission.

The new principle of a zoning bonus for plazas proved far more popular with developers than had been anticipated; but the use of the plaza bonus, by itself, has created some serious design problems of its own. While plazas have introduced valuable open space into the city, their proliferation has accentuated some of the defects of the underlying zoning, notably the tendency of the regulations to separate each new building from its surroundings. Beneath the language specifying setbacks, plazas, and open-space ratios are certain assumptions about what the resulting buildings should look like. Unfortunately, these implied architectural standards are based upon the "revolutionary" concepts of architecture expounded by Le Corbusier and others during the 1920s. Their vision of the city of the future

Le Corbusier's all-too-prophetic drawing, from the first English edition of *Towards a New Architecture,* published in 1927.

as a park filled with orderly rows of towers of the same design and height does not seem to be adaptable to zoning and the implementation of different-sized buildings on a lot-by-lot basis.

Zoning regulations that encourage plazas have had the effect of belatedly imposing a fragmentary version of 1920s modernism on cities, creating towers that stand in their individual pools of plaza space, surrounded by the party walls of earlier structures that were planned to face the street. Shopping frontages are interrupted and open spaces appear at random, unrelated to topography, sunlight, or the design of the plaza across the way.

Le Corbusier's revolutionary vision assumed that the encumbrances of the past could be swept away, and cities could rise again in an entirely new form. But the process inaugurated by New York City's 1961 zoning ordinance or San Francisco's ordinance of 1966 would take forty or more years to implement. Eventually, New York would indeed become a city of towers and open space, but a city whose elements were inevitably random and accidental. No matter how well the individual buildings were designed, the city itself would have no design at all.

The elements of New York City built before 1961 do follow certain design criteria. Simple-minded as they may seem, uniform cornice lines and facades that followed the street gave the city some coherence. The old zoning rules created dreary courts and light wells, errors that the new law corrects; but the continuity that the pre-1961 zoning imposed on the street was a virtue that was not appreciated until it was already lost.

Because the plaza (not to be confused with a real plaza, a European town square) was the major incentive provision in 1960s' zoning ordinances, it has come to have an excessively important role in the design of the city. After all, plazas, as defined by zoning, while they make a pleasant addition to the cityscape, have limited usefulness in a northern climate, and even more limited usefulness when they are not part of a coordinated open-space plan.

In the highly complex central areas of a city, the plaza should be one element in a designed pattern of pedestrian and traffic movement. Other necessary elements include shopping arcades, covered pedestrian spaces (like the enclosed malls found in some suburban shopping centers), elevated walkways and underground concourses to allow the separation of pedestrians and traffic, and off-street loading docks to help eliminate traffic tie-ups.

The nature of the activities permitted by zoning is also important. Zoning traditionally has separated land uses into distinct zones. But downtown centers should have a desirable mix of activities, so that there are interesting places for office workers to shop and to have lunch, and some housing in the vicinity so that the area does not become dead as soon as the office workers go home. Continuous activity not only makes the city safer but ensures better use of essential services, utilities, fire and police protection, and so on. A variety of activities also creates a reinforcement phenomenon: in urban planning, or real estate, two and two often add up to five or six.

The 1961 zoning resolution does not provide a satisfactory set of rules for New York City's intensively used central business districts, and similar regulations in other American cities have similar problems. Not only should new buildings be placed so that they do not block each other's light and air; they should also be part of a coherent, planned set of relationships that are both architectural and functional, and equally meaningful whether composed entirely of new buildings or a mixture of old and new.

Zoning incentives on a building-by-building basis cannot supply the planned set of relationships required in the complex central districts of a city, although they are effective in less complicated, and less intensely developed, areas.

A further technique, in addition to planned unit development, urban renewal controls, and zoning incentives, was needed as a means of designing cities. Some of the special zoning districts developed in New York City use new forms of legal controls that should represent an improvement in the administration of urban renewal as well as zoning. These special districts are the subject of the next chapter.

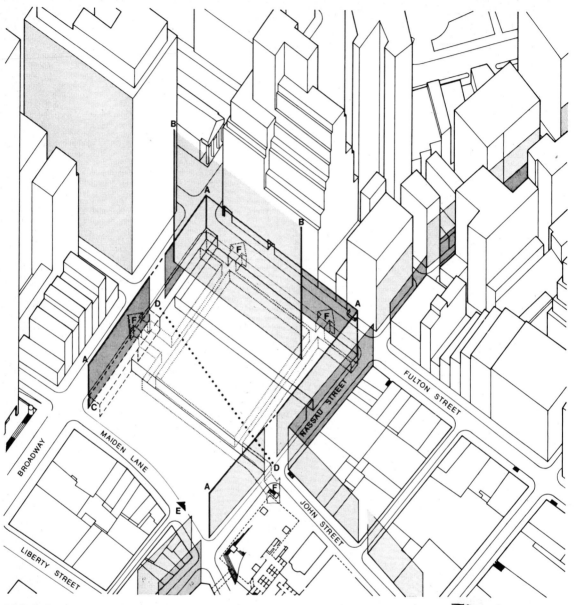

NASSAU-FULTON

A Build-to line at lot line, 85 foot height mandatory.
B Build-to plane, parallel to the south face of the AT&T building.
C Arcade along Broadway.
D Through circulation between John Street and Dey Street.
E Access to parking and loading below grade.
F Arrows (dotted line) indicate primary locations of subway
   entrances at concourse level.

0   80   160

DESIGNING CITIES WITHOUT DESIGNING BUILDINGS

6

The Evolution of
New York City's
Special Zoning Districts

The first attempt by New York City to extend zoning
regulation to encompass new urban design and planning objectives came in response to the invasion of the
traditional midtown Manhattan theater district by
large, modern office towers. I have described this experience in detail in *Urban Design as Public Policy,* and
will only repeat the essential elements of the story here.

A proposed office building for the site of the old
Astor Hotel on the west side of Times Square became
a test case through which the New York City Planning
Commission—aided by its then (1967) newly established urban design staff—sought to create an urban
design and development policy for the whole theater
district.

Although there were no existing theaters on the
Astor Hotel site, the Planning Commission asked the
developer to build a new legitimate theater. The commission had bargaining power because the developer
was seeking a special permit that would allow the building's tower portion to be somewhat larger than the 40
percent of the lot area permitted by right.

The developer said that the suggestion of building a
theater was ridiculous and went around the Planning
Commission to Mayor Lindsay. Lindsay backed the
commission and its chairman, Donald Elliott. The developer then said that, if the city wanted a theater, it
would have to permit a much larger building than was
possible under existing zoning laws.

The Theater District

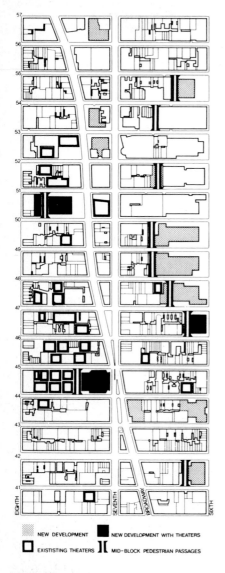

NEW DEVELOPMENT NEW DEVELOPMENT WITH THEATERS

EXISTISTING THEATERS MID-BLOCK PEDESTRIAN PASSAGES

Map of the Theater District, showing existing theaters and the three buildings (containing four theaters) that have been built so far under the incentive zoning for the district.

After negotiation, the Planning Commission determined that a 20 percent larger tower was a legitimate form of compensation for the costs of building a theater —costs that could not be paid for out of the income the theater would generate.

The Planning Commission's counsel, Norman Marcus, suggested that a special district was a means by which it would be possible to grant a developer a 20 percent larger building. The Special Theater District legislation covered the area between 40th and 57th Streets, from Eighth Avenue to the Avenue of the Americas. Within these boundaries, the developer could make an application for a special permit to increase the floor area of a building up to 20 percent in return for building a legitimate theater that met the Planning Commission's specifications. The size of the floor-area bonus and the characteristics of the theater were both matters of negotiation between the developer and the Planning Commission.

One lesson from the Theater District experience was that the preservation of valuable functions of the city and the creation of desirable amenities can be achieved if you can find a way to make them profitable, or at least break-even, ventures.

Another lesson was that zoning not only can provide the solution, but was a large part of the problem in the first place. The segregation of land uses implicit in the concept of zoning is not as appropriate to a complex central business district as it is in the outskirts of the city. True, you don't want any chemical factories downtown; but you do want to encourage diversity and complexity.

The whole subject of zoning was a revelation to the urban designers working for the City Planning Department at that time. As a result of our experience with the Theater District, we came to realize that zoning could be made into one of the basic methods of designing cities.

The Theater District became the first in a series of which the Lincoln Square, Fifth Avenue, Greenwich Street, and Lower Manhattan special districts were probably the most important.

DESIGNING CITIES WITHOUT DESIGNING BUILDINGS

The Theater District was also a revelation to New York City's real estate developers. It showed them that zoning regulations might be subject to negotiation. The result was to add a new element to the way the real estate business operates in New York. In each of the special districts, individual proposals had signaled the need to reconsider land-use controls for a particular area, and negotiations with a developer were used as a test case for the new controls. The intent was to create an improved set of regulations, which would then operate without additional new legislation and would require the minimum of individual, ad hoc decision making. The problem was that negotiation, while it was useful medicine, turned out to be addictive.

While the special districts were providing new solutions to some old problems, the means by which they were created was thus causing a new problem, the Negotiation Syndrome, which we will come back to in Chapter 7. First, however, let us look at the evolution of the most significant special districts.

The Theater District legislation had set up a framework for negotiation between each individual developer and the Planning Commission. Because the design of theaters involves so many complexities and variables, it would have been difficult to draft any other kind of legislation for the district. Its special permit procedure has drawbacks, however. It allows the city government considerable discretion, which makes it difficult for the public to be certain that it knows what is going on. From the developer's point of view, having to pass a separate piece of legislation for each theater is a cumbersome and uncertain process. Each special permit, under the city charter adopted in 1976, is subject to the Uniform Land Use Review Procedure—known familiarly as ULURP. This requires a hearing and recommendation by the appropriate Community Planning Board, and then still requires that each special permit be passed by both the Planning Commission and the Board of Estimate, meaning two more public hearings and several months in which the developer does not know how large the building is going to be.

Case-by-case decisions cannot be entirely eliminated

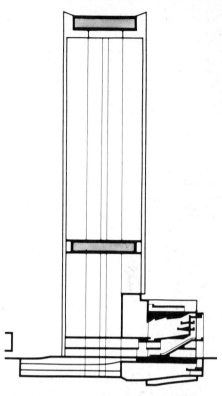

A section through the One Astor Plaza building shows the location of the theater and the way the lobby areas look out over Times Square.

Photo of the One Astor Plaza building from Times Square showing the glass-walled lobbies from the outside. The architects were Kahn & Jacobs; Der Scutt, project designer.

The Lincoln Square District

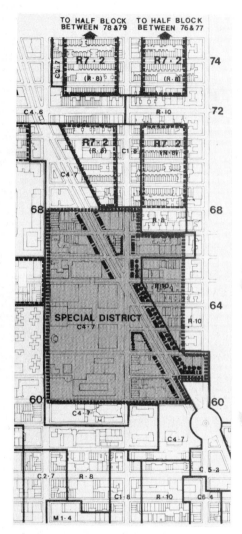

The Lincoln Square Special Zoning District shapes private development in the area surrounding the Lincoln Center for the Performing Arts.

from the administration of zoning, but each New York special district enacted after the Theater District legislation set forth complex urban design objectives that could be administered in much the same way as conventional zoning requirements. They did not require a reprise of the legislative process every time a new building was approved. It is the method of setting down urban design objectives in zoning language that makes these zoning districts significant, even if their full importance has not been appreciated by the New York City Planning Commission itself.

The Lincoln Square Special Zoning District, which was the second of the incentive districts and was passed directly following the Theater District legislation, contained the first language that specified a range of mandated or optional improvements in advance of any decision to build. Its purpose was to regulate the development of new buildings in the neighborhood of the Lincoln Center for the Performing Arts. One of the subsidiary purposes of Lincoln Center had been to stimulate private real estate development; but there was no master plan for this development, much less any means of seeing that a plan was followed.

The Lincoln Square District provides such a plan. The lower floors of the buildings fronting on Broadway are required to go out to the building line. This "build-to" line is the analogue of the more traditional zoning setback lines. An arcade along the Broadway frontage is also mandated, and compensated by a small floor-area bonus. The plaza, if the developer wishes to build one, must therefore be along the mid-blocks rather than on Broadway. The incentive provisions permit a 20 percent larger floor area over the maximum permitted in a residential zone, but this additional space is commercial space.

Another interesting provision of the Lincoln Square District is that the "use-group," which specifies the permissible ground-floor shops along Broadway, has been written to encourage small shops and restaurants and prevent a high percentage of this space being rented by banks or other uses that would not operate at night, when Lincoln Center is open.

The Fifth Avenue Special Zoning District represents an advance, from a conceptual and technical point of view, over Lincoln Square. Like the new zoning for the theater district, its basic intention was conservative. In this case, it was the department stores and other retail shops along Fifth Avenue that were in need of protection.

To a visitor strolling along Fifth Avenue, the substantial limestone buildings may seem some of the most permanent things imaginable. To a real estate developer, the view is quite different. With a map of the underlying zoning in mind, the developer knows that many sites along the Avenue are "soft"; that is, the zoning would permit a far larger building than is there right now. Although Fifth Avenue is midtown's most expensive land, the demand for office space makes it economic to redevelop, which had not been anticipated when the underlying zoning map was drawn in 1961.

A shopping street has a delicate web of interconnecting relationships. Sever the web in one or two places, and a whole commercial district may die. This is the reason why suburban shopping centers are always planned with the small stores situated on the routes that link the major stores. Centers that break this rule have usually failed; in fact, the arrangement of leases in a shopping center can mean the difference between success and failure.

On a street like Fifth Avenue, the arrangement of stores has been an evolutionary process; stores that were in the wrong place have failed, or moved, and the resulting complex of shops is there because it works well in that form. If real estate considerations not related to retailing were to dictate that a substantial portion of the street become plaza space, or banks and airline ticket offices, there would be a powerful adverse effect on the rest of the stores.

The nearly simultaneous decision of two department stores to close their doors and sell out to real estate interests alarmed both the Fifth Avenue Association and the Planning Commission. The two stores, Best & Co. and DePinna, were situated diagonally across the Avenue from each other, just north of St. Patrick's

Maps describe some of the provisions of the Fifth Avenue Special Zoning District. The buildings outlined as "soft" are those judged likely to be redeveloped at some time.

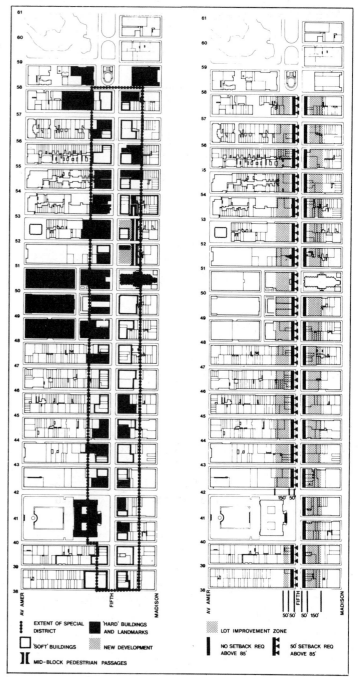

DESIGNING CITIES WITHOUT DESIGNING BUILDINGS

Cathedral and Rockefeller Center, in the heart of the midtown area.

It was feared that the withdrawal of two such important sites from retail use would have very serious consequences. After several months of intensive study, Jaquelin Robertson, then director of the Mayor's Office of Midtown Planning and Development, presented a Fifth Avenue Special Zoning District for review by the various midtown interest groups; and, following the appropriate public hearing process, the plan became law, adopted with overwhelming support. This was the first zoning law in the United States that encouraged a mix of residences, offices, and shops in single buildings of the downtown office district. It thus represents a major innovation in land-use policy and a model for other cities now trapped into single-use, eight-hour-a-day downtowns.

The Fifth Avenue District covers the frontage along the Avenue from 38th to 57th Streets, with regulations affecting an area 200 feet deep on either side. The ground-floor frontages are reserved for the specified retail uses, excluding airline ticket offices and banks. To strengthen window-shopping continuity, the frontage cannot be broken with office entrances; and development on both sides of the Avenue must hold to the building line to a height of 85 feet. On the east side of the Avenue, the tower portion of the building may continue straight up from the building line—a feature designed to preserve the existing "wall" of Fifth Avenue (see page 63)—while, to preserve an appropriate distance between office towers, buildings above the 85-foot line on the west side of the Avenue must be set back 50 feet. Plazas, if they occur, must be back from the Avenue, and developers are encouraged to substitute covered "galleria" space for the plazas. Office entrances and smaller, low-rental shops would be in the galleria. The regulations are drawn so that most of them can be followed by the developer "as of right."

The bonus provisions for this district promote mixed use, but in the reverse of the proportions at Lincoln Square. The developer can add up to 20 percent more floor space to his building by carrying out the provisions of the district, but this extra space must be used for apartments, not offices.

This provision helps answer a criticism of special districts with zoning incentives: that the amenities and more complex land uses obtained are valuable, but that the city cannot afford to keep purchasing them at the expense of increased density.

Residential and office uses are to a large extent complementary, in that they cause their peak loads on the city's service infrastructure at different times of the day. Twenty-four-hour use, created by placing offices and apartments in the same district, makes that portion of the city safer and more efficient than an office building area that is deserted at night, or an in-town residential neighborhood that empties out during the day. The same police and fire stations can serve both, as can the same shops and restaurants, and the streets remain active at all hours, which is a good defense against crime.

The Fifth Avenue District not only helps preserve the integrity of a major shopping street, but it is introducing a wider variety of uses into the area; and the new shopping arcades create new kinds of frontage, encouraging a wider variety of stores. A downtown composed solely of office buildings and parking lots is not desirable either to the citizen or the real estate developer. Further, in New York as in many other places, the very zoning regulations that were meant to safeguard the public interest were helping to change the business district into an area that lacked the variety and liveliness that is one of the city's major advantages. Purchasing twenty-four-hour use by incentives that create building bulk has proved controversial, however. We will see in Chapter 7 that the city has decided to remove the bonus for residential use in the Fifth Avenue District as part of a general reaction against large new buildings in midtown.

The Greenwich Street Special District was created to control redevelopment in a segment of lower Manhattan. In many ways it is as ambitious as an urban renewal plan, but the plan is to be carried out solely thorough the medium of zoning. Unlike urban renewal, there is no way to control which parcel will be devel-

DESIGNING CITIES WITHOUT DESIGNING BUILDINGS

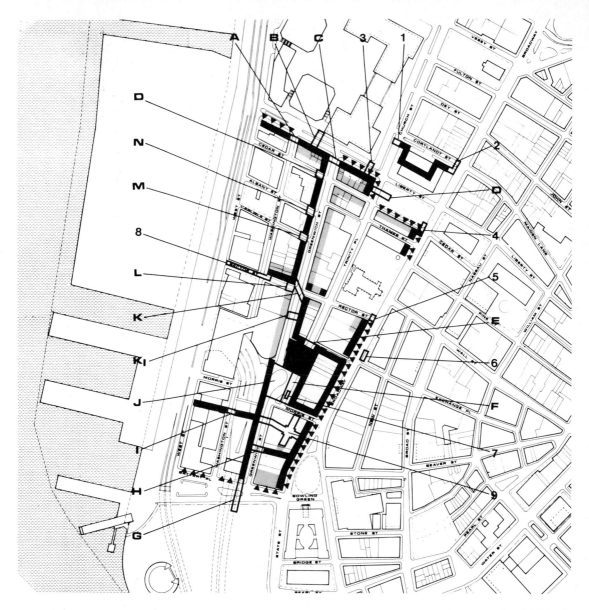

Map of Greenwich Street Special District
shows mandatory and elective
improvements based on a predetermined
design plan.

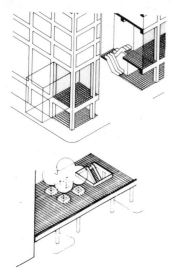

These drawings are part of the official description of improvements that are rewarded with bonus points in the Greenwich Street District.

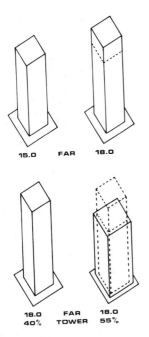

The developer's reward can take the form of increased tower coverage, as well as bonus floor area.

oped at what time, or even to know if certain portions of the area will ever be redeveloped at all.

The Greenwich Street District required that the urban designers, working under the direction of Richard Weinstein, who was then the director of the Office of Lower Manhattan Development, would determine which were the most significant design issues in the area. Then Edgar Lampert, at that time counsel to the Development Offices, translated these design requirements into zoning language.

The most important design issue turned out to be the movement of people through the district, as the size of the buildings that could be permitted is a function of the amount of congestion that the occupants and the necessary services would create.

A circulation plan was drawn up, showing the best possible movement pattern to improve access to the subways, and to make traffic and people move more smoothly at street level. In addition, an upper-level pedestrian shopping concourse was planned, with bridges connecting the buildings to the plaza level of the World Trade Center on the north, and to the plaza level of Battery Park City, a major housing development already planned for the landfill in the Hudson River immediately to the west of the special district.

Each block was then studied separately to determine which improvements were essential if the overall plan were to work, and which additional elements were desirable, if the developer wished to create them.

Each improvement was given a clear definition: underground concourses, arcades, galleries, loggias, plazas, and several different types of pedestrian bridges. These items, which all add to the developer's costs, were given a bonus value in floor area, on the same principle as the floor-area bonus for plazas that had been created for the 1961 zoning revision. The increased rental from the larger building offsets the cost of the improvements. In some cases, the developer is permitted to construct a building that covers a larger percentage of the site than the 40 percent tower coverage usually permitted. Short, fat buildings are cheaper

DESIGNING CITIES WITHOUT DESIGNING BUILDINGS

to construct than tall, thin buildings, so this concession is the equivalent of a bonus and is treated as such. It is possible to loosen the bulk restrictions and still follow sound planning principles because, within the district, the location of buildings and their relationships have to a large degree been planned in advance.

There are also some mandatory provisions that do not necessarily involve additional cost, which are designed to preserve the continuity of the streetscape by holding building and cornice lines.

The need to put the whole Greenwich Street plan into legal language forced the designers to define exactly what their most important objectives were. All the provisions were designed to be self-administering, without discretionary decisions by the City Planning Commission. Although the building that is now the Bankers Trust Company Building provided the test case and was the subject of negotiation and discussion, the intent of the district was that no such negotiation would be required again. A property owner can look up a lot in the zoning text, and see both what improvements are required and what other elements may be added to increase the size of the building up to the limit specified in the regulations.

As a result, the Greenwich Street zoning text becomes both lengthy and complicated, particularly in the language dealing with improvements connecting one building to another, as the second building may not be constructed for years.

In some cases, owners can receive a bonus for contributions to improvements that do not connect directly to their property at all. In the event that these elements are not ready to be constructed, the developer makes a cash contribution to an escrow fund, the amount of the contribution being based on an index derived from the assessed value of sixty office buildings. The index is revised annually according to a formula that is part of the district legislation.

In addition to the incentives and controls regulating floor area, the text of the district contains rules for land uses that ensure variety in the retail spaces along the

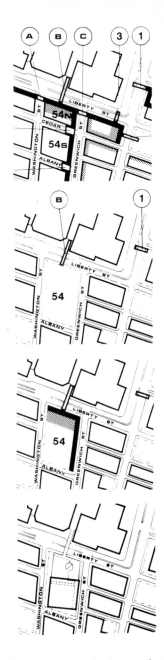

The developer of a particular parcel can look up that location in the zoning book and find out just what the requirements are.

How a key parcel at the north end of the
Greenwich Street District relates to the
World Trade Center.

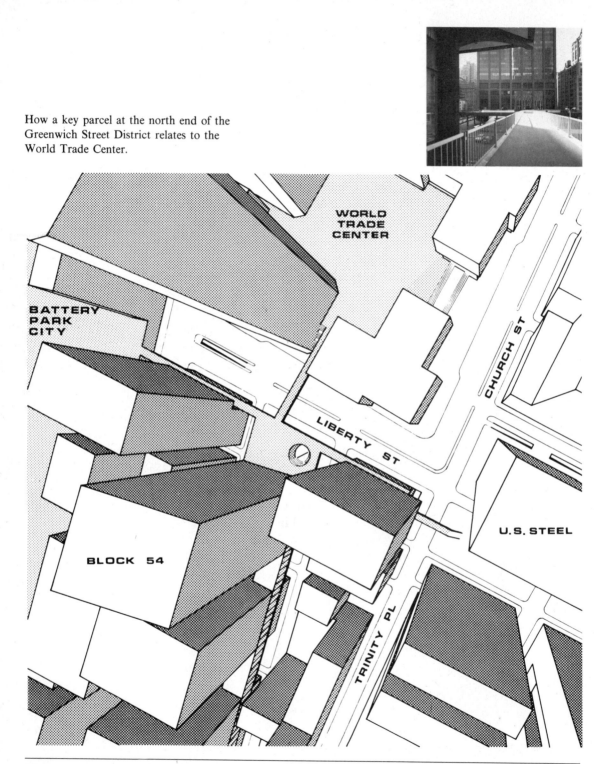

DESIGNING CITIES WITHOUT DESIGNING BUILDINGS

concourses, preventing them from being preempted by high-paying but boring tenants like banks and airline ticket offices.

One of the architects designing a building in the Greenwich Street District found, to his surprise, that he could not do the tower surrounded by plaza space that had become the usual formula for the "prestige" office structure. He was outraged at such interference with his artistic prerogatives, particularly when he discovered that he was up against a law, which could only be amended by the Planning Commission and the Board of Estimate. The creativity of the individual architect is subordinated to the design of the district. This principle had been debated and accepted by New York architects when the New York chapter of the American Institute of Architects supported the passage of the Lincoln Square Special District.

The most complicated special zoning districts of all were those that extended the principle of look-it-up-in-the-zoning-book urban design to the landfill areas around the periphery of lower Manhattan. These districts were called the Manhattan Landing and Battery Park City special districts, and were also worked out under the direction of Richard Weinstein and Edgar Lampert.

The Lower Manhattan special districts were related to the earlier Lower Manhattan Plan drawn up by Wallace, McHarg Associates and Conklin & Rossant. But while the Lower Manhattan Plan was expressed in the traditional illustrative site drawing shown on page 90, the special districts undertook to identify the essential design elements and express them in legal language.

These design elements were defined as:

Design Continuity
Visual Corridors
Visual Permeability.

Based on these concepts, a text and illustrative drawings were devised to control the essential aspects of the new development without prescribing the design of the buildings.

Historically, lower Manhattan has always grown by

The Lower Manhattan Districts

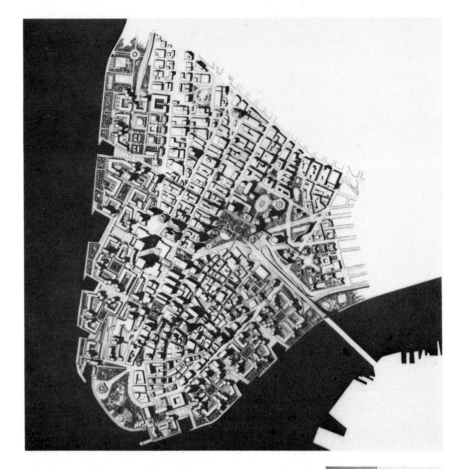

These two maps are traditional illustrative site plans meant to show what development will look like when everything is completed at some indefinite time in the future. Above: the Lower Manhattan Plan drawn by Wallace, McHarg Associates, Conklin & Rossant, and Alan M. Voorhees Associates. Right: a later version of part of the same plan, Battery Park City, drawn by a team of architects that included the firms of Harrison & Abramovitz, Conklin & Rossant, and Philip Johnson & John Burgee.

landfill, with the existing street system being extended. The result was the automatic integration of new development with old.

For the latest landfill, it was clearly not necessary to extend all the streets, whose spacing had originally been set in the seventeenth century; but it would also be undesirable to have the new buildings on the landfill totally unrelated to the patterns created in the past. The problem was further complicated by the existence of an elevated highway that loops around all of lower Manhattan at what was, at the time it was built, the water's edge. The original Lower Manhattan Plan had dealt with the highway by proposing that it be rebuilt below grade. It is unlikely that the highway on the East River side will be rebuilt for many years, although the plan for the new Westway puts the highway underground on the Battery Park City side. Design continuity is easier there than on the East Side, where it becomes a complicated three-dimensional problem with the need for connections over and under the elevated structure.

The zoning district, and the revised lease provisions for Battery Park City, selected certain streets as significant for design continuity, and required that their forms be carried on into new development. In addition, the controls ask recognition of the geometry established by certain major buildings in lower Manhattan that are likely to be in existence for a long time.

The controls establish visual corridors, which define areas that should be left clear of buildings, but also create planes that the buildings must come up to: both open space and the planes of buildings defining the space are specified. An esplanade is also defined, which will give the public the ability to walk freely along the entire waterfront.

Because the most significant experience of the new buildings would be that of people walking to them, the controls seek to regulate buildings in terms of that experience. A percentage of the esplanade, and, to a more limited extent, the visual corridors, may be penetrated by buildings that are visually permeable—if the ground floor of the building is left open, for example.

The nature of this kind of planning can be studied in

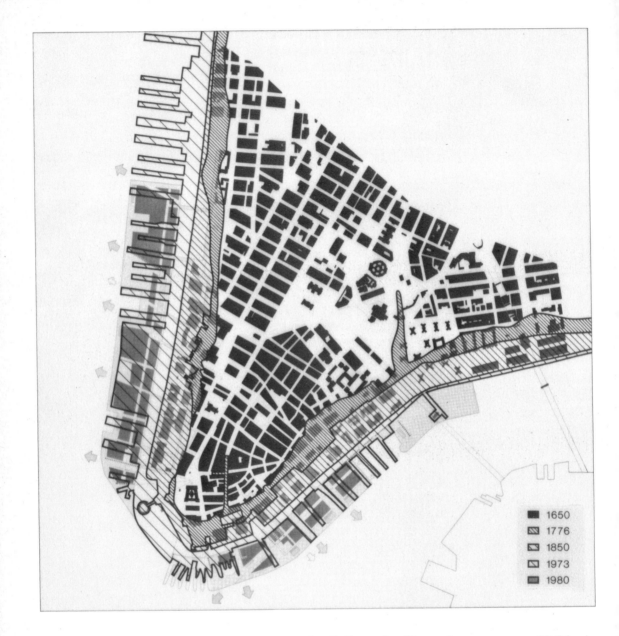

■	1650
▨	1776
▩	1850
▨	1973
▨	1980

Composite map of lower Manhattan by the Office of Lower Manhattan Development, showing how the area has been enlarged by successive landfills.

more detail from the illustrations on pages 92-96. As the illustrations show, the design policies for the landfill relate to the design concept for the Greenwich Street District and other inland areas, so that the ensemble was a comprehensive plan for lower Manhattan.

The city government seeks to define only those elements of concern to the public, leaving the developer to

DESIGNING CITIES WITHOUT DESIGNING BUILDINGS

operate at will within these clearly stated constraints.

The elements of the plan are tied back into the pre-existing fabric of lower Manhattan, both functionally and visually, so that the large new additions to this part of the city would help form the whole Lower Manhattan district into a single, unified design.

At the same time, the nature of the design controls

Present building masses in lower Manhattan, from the same drawing sequence as illustration opposite.

The next map in the series shows the location of existing and proposed buildings and view corridors that extend existing streets. If these view corridors are to be maintained, new buildings must be confined to the areas shown. This principle underlay the illustrative site plans on page 90, but is here expressed as a principle rather than developed as an architectural illustration.

permits the design to make sense as each increment is added; and they are sufficiently flexible to allow for different types of buildings as time goes on.

The Theater District, followed by the Lincoln Square, Fifth Avenue, Greenwich Street, and Lower Manhattan special districts, are a progression of increasingly sophisticated urban design controls, which

help answer a fundamental question of large-scale planning and design: How do you design cities without designing buildings?

Master plans have generally been either too explicit or not explicit enough. A typical urban renewal plan is simply a map of designated land uses, with the renewal area divided into parcels. Each parcel has its own spon-

The zoning districts adopted for the lower Manhattan perimeter required that visual corridors not only be left open but defined by new construction, through the use of "build-to" lines.

The zoning controls defined in the previous
illustration are shown here overlaying the
masses of existing buildings.

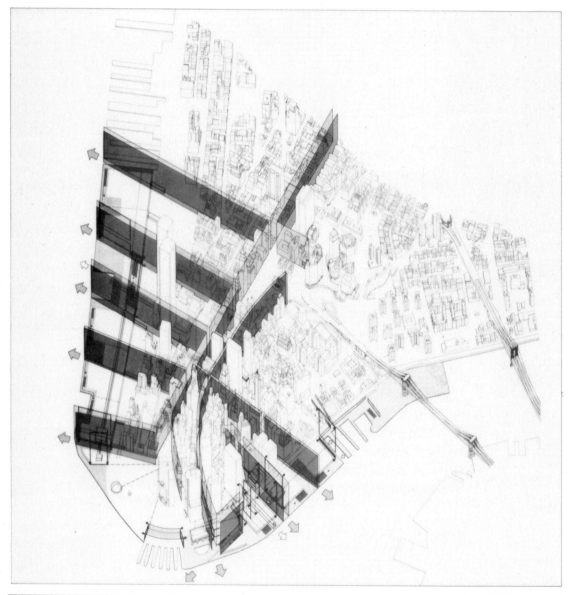

DESIGNING CITIES WITHOUT DESIGNING BUILDINGS

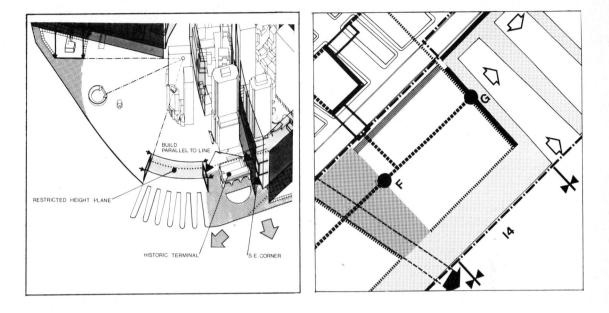

sor and architect, and it is no one's job to design the whole district.

Alternatively, there can be a very explicit architectural model, with all the individual buildings carefully arranged, every tree and path put in with loving attention to detail. Such models give the impression that all the buildings have been designed, but nothing of the sort has happened: the sponsors and architects have generally not even been selected at this point. If the renewal plan is written so that design controls follow the model, the chances are that the controls will have to be amended later, on a case-by-case basis. The result is likely to be a series of compromises that may well be worse than no plan at all.

Seeking to design all the buildings at the master planning stage is an unnecessarily cumbersome as well as ineffective technique. The planner is put in rather the same position as Charles Lamb's farmer, whose house had burned down, roasting his pig, which had been caught in the conflagration. His neighbors acquired a taste for roast pig; ever after, on village feast days, the farmer was asked to put a pig in a house and burn it down.

More detailed illustrations of the lower Manhattan special districts show how legal controls seek to define salient points of public interest while leaving the architecture to the developer and architect.

Development controls at the Historic South Street Seaport.

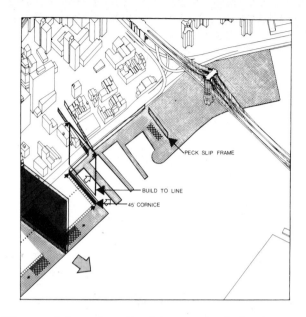

PECK SLIP FRAME

BUILD TO LINE

45° CORNICE

An answer to the question: How do you design cities without designing buildings?

The special zoning districts, particularly the more complex districts created for lower Manhattan, seemed to be a way of roasting pigs without burning down the house. If you understand the salient points of the overall design, know exactly which ones are most crucial, and understand the steps required to make sure that what is important will actually be done, then you do not need to design the individual buildings in detail in order to ensure that the overall concept will be carried out.

So much for the theory; but what has actually happened in practice? To evaluate the special zoning districts it is necessary to understand the negotiation addiction, and the importance of the tower regulations, which are usually what brought the developer to the negotiating table and often meant more than the prospect of an increase in the overall floor space. This evaluation is the subject of the next chapter.

7

Comprehensive Policies to Replace Special Zoning Districts

During the 1970s, the urban design mechanisms created by some of New York City's special zoning districts had shown themselves to be moderately successful; but the city became addicted to creating new zoning provisions, taking them almost to the point of a one-sentence zoning law: "The Planning Commission shall permit such development as, from time to time, it considers to be appropriate."

The One-Sentence Zoning Resolution

What happened to special zoning districts was a little like what happened to penicillin. When penicillin was first introduced, it acquired a reputation as a "miracle drug" and was prescribed in many situations for which it was not appropriate. Then people became disillusioned with penicillin; not only was it often unsuccessful, but various strains of disease became resistant to it. Penicillin lost its reputation for miracles, although it continues to be a useful antibiotic.

The Penicillin Effect

Something of the same thing seems to be happening to the perception of special zoning districts and other innovative zoning provisions. Since the Theater District was enacted in 1968, New York City has enacted thirty more special zoning districts. Some, like the Brooklyn Heights Limited Building Height District (for an area of historic houses), are non-controversial and sensible. Others have had relatively little influence. The objectives are always laudable, but a special zoning district may not have been the right prescription in all cases.

The Negotiation Syndrome

Each of the special design districts described in the previous chapter had been established by negotiation with a specific developer or developers; but the situation was supposed to be prototypical. The concerns of one entrepreneur were likely to be similar to others intending to build in the same district, and what was feasible for one would be practicable for all. Unfortunately, negotiation has attractions of its own.

If a developer can buy a piece of property at a price that anticipates one level of development and, through negotiation, can change the zoning category to permit a larger or more valuable form of development, you can be sure the developer will try to do it. Changing land value is, of course, the traditional way in which money is made in real estate. What the Theater District did was to create a precedent for a new form of negotiation.

Developers love negotiation. Not only is it the way they make money; there is something about the process that appeals to the temperament of people who go into real estate development in the first place. Ostensibly the developer is saying: "Just tell us what the rules are and leave us alone." Each special zoning district became more complicated than the last in order to operate "as of right," no negotiation. But, if the stakes are high enough, developers are more than willing to give up the advantages of the known quantity in favor of trying to negotiate a better deal.

Evidently city planners love negotiation also. The evolution of the special urban design districts took place in the context of a continuous series of changes in the entire zoning law.

When I left New York City government in 1971, the Planning Commission was still in what might be called the classic phase of zoning amendment. This phase was followed—as the historians tell us it would be—by a mannerist phase, and then a period of baroque elaboration. When a 1977 staff study stopped to count up the changes in the zoning resolution since the comprehensive revisions adopted in 1961, it turned out that the zoning resolution had grown from 937 sections to 2,131, and only 27 percent of the current total had remained unchanged since 1961. Sixteen percent of the

DESIGNING CITIES WITHOUT DESIGNING BUILDINGS

added sections had themselves been amended since they were adopted. In addition to these text changes, there were about 1,200 map changes during the same period.

New York City is a big place and no one believes that land-use regulations should be immutable. Nevertheless, the city has compiled a remarkable record of, well, flexibility. Many of the new sections of New York City's zoning regulations that have been included in this book because of their significance to the practice of urban design represent valuable innovations. In addition to some of the special zoning districts, there are the housing quality regulations described on pages 220–221, and the improved plaza regulations described on page 179.

However, there is another large category of zoning change that results from what we can call the Negotiation Syndrome. Ostensibly of general application, these changes have been carefully drafted to apply only to a limited set of circumstances and have been passed to permit a particular structure to be built.

In such a climate, it is not surprising that developers would try to negotiate even the basic requirements of special zoning districts that, ironically, had been designed to protect developers from the delays created by government decision making by making provisions "as of right." We see a remarkable case of the syndrome at work in 1979 when the New York City Planning Commission prepared new language, and held a public hearing, on a zoning amendment that would permit the owner of a building in the Fifth Avenue Special District *to rent the covered pedestrian public space as a department store.* The building had already been completed, the building had received a bonus of 20 percent additional floor area for providing the interior public space, and the Planning Commission showed itself willing to consider letting the owner rent out this public space for a highly profitable use. If the prime office tenant hadn't objected strenuously, the commission might well have gone ahead with the amendment.

In another matter considered at the same time, the commission would have permitted a developer to build a row of stores on a plaza, again in a situation where construction was complete and the bonus for the plaza had produced a larger building. Perhaps the commission realized that this action might open the door to new structures on every zoning plaza in the city; in any event, it drew back after the hearing.

Had the atmosphere of constant negotiation and amendment caused New York City's Planning Commission to lose sight of the basic principles of zoning? To answer this question, we need to examine the Trojan Horse Corollary.

When the lawyers for the owner began negotiating to change the covered pedestrian space into a department store, they did not present their argument in terms of zoning. What they said was, in effect: "Which would you rather have: a useless public space that nobody wants anyway, or a vibrant department store strengthening the retail district and providing additional tax revenue to the city?" Similarly, the presentation of the stores on the plaza went something like this: "Instead of this dangerous open space (with evil criminals lurking behind every tree) that the law forces us to build, you could have this row of lively neighborhood stores adding convenience and safety to your streets." In addition, the developer expressed willingness to make a cash contribution to a nearby city park: "You can have your park and your stores as well." The Community Planning Board found these arguments convincing; so did the staff of the City Planning Department.

In this way the Trojan Horse Corollary is added to the Negotiation Syndrome. Nobody mentioned the possibility that a public space could be as vibrant as a department store and that the store could find an equally good site in another building and would still return tax revenue to the city. In fact it turned out that the store was negotiating with another developer, and had probably promoted the zoning amendment as a ploy in its own negotiation. Similarly, public outdoor spaces can be designed so that evil criminals do not lurk; it is not necessary to build stores in order to make the city safe, if indeed stores do promote safety. In any case, if authorities no longer desire public plazas, the logical thing to do is stop giving bonuses for them.

The Trojan Horse Corollary

DESIGNING CITIES WITHOUT DESIGNING BUILDINGS

The Trojan Horse arguments were cunningly devised to conceal the central issue: the substantial additional floor area that the developer had already received in return for benefits that now were to be taken back.

Another aspect of the Trojan Horse Corollary is to provide valuable benefits for the owner in the name of good design, usually sanctified by the use of a famous architect.

The 1961 zoning ordinance provided that a tower could occupy no more than 40 percent of a site going up from a line 80 feet above street level. In order to deal with cases where the logic of the structure or the dimensions of the site made the 40 percent limit too restrictive, the zoning gave the Planning Commission the power to make minor variations. Buildings that are not towers are expected to set back from the building line on the higher floors, their bulk confined by an imaginary line known as the "sky-exposure plane." Exceptions to the tower regulations are thus called modifications to height and setback regulations, or permitted infractions of the sky-exposure plane.

These changes are not variances but are created through the piece of legislation known as a special permit. It is a discretionary action, a matter of negotiation between the Planning Commission and the developer. Over a period of time, these permits modifying coverage and allowing invasion of the sky-exposure plane have become less and less minor until they have become total.

The sequence begins within special zoning districts like the Fifth Avenue and the Greenwich Street, where major changes in the usual setback regulations were permitted as part of the overall concept of the district. For example, Olympic Tower, a building in the Fifth Avenue District, is permitted to go straight up from the building line on the Fifth Avenue side (a 100 percent infraction of the sky-exposure plane) because the buildings on the other side of Fifth Avenue are to be set back in accordance with the district provisions. Olympic Tower is also permitted to cover all of its site, because it provides a covered pedestrian space instead of an outdoor plaza.

Above is the pedestrian space of the AT&T Building.

The next step was to give similar concessions to buildings that were not in special districts. The IBM Building at the corner of 57th Street and Madison Avenue, designed by Edward L. Barnes, goes straight up from the building line on both faces of the corner. It is, however, set back on the third side to make room for an elegant covered pedestrian space, which is a branch of the Bronx Botanic Garden. IBM, except for its 100 percent invasion of the sky-exposure plane, conforms to the usual zoning requirements: its tower occupies 40 percent of the site.

Directly to the south of IBM is the AT&T Building by Philip Johnson & John Burgee. It goes straight up from the building line on three sides, and its tower occupies 55 percent of the site. There is irony in the fact that AT&T blocks most of the sunlight from IBM's Botanic Garden. The rationale behind permitting IBM to violate the sky-exposure plane had been to permit the

From left to right: the IBM Building by Edward L. Barnes & Partners—part of a series of new buildings in New York City in which existing bulk controls were loosened progressively until they ceased to exist. The IBM Building is a 40 percent tower, as the zoning requires, but breaks the sky-exposure plane regulations almost completely on two streets.

The AT&T Building by Philip Johnson & John Burgee is next in this series. It is a 55 percent tower, and creates 100 percent infractions of the sky-exposure plane regulations on three streets. In addition, the floor-to-floor distances are unusually high, creating the impression of a bulkier building than the zoning permits.

499 Park Avenue, by I. M. Pei & Partners, an 80 percent tower, with 100 percent infractions of the sky-exposure plane on two streets.

The Philip Morris Building, by Ulrich Franzen & Associates, a 100 percent tower and 100 percent infractions of the sky-exposure plane on three streets.

Botanic Garden to occupy the south side of the site. AT&T is then brought forward on its site to match IBM and, allegedly, to minimize sun blockage for the Garden.

Now let us consider 499 Park, designed by I. M. Pei & Partners. It was permitted by the Board of Standards and Appeals to invade the sky-exposure plane fully on both frontages and its tower occupies 80 percent of the site. Last in this sequence is the Philip Morris Building by Ulrich Franzen. Its tower occupies 100 percent of the site and it invades the sky-exposure plane fully on all three street frontages.

These are four excellent pieces of architecture, and each has a ground-floor pedestrian space that is of real benefit to the public. However, they represent a sequence in which traditional zoning restraints have been set aside. Does it matter?

Well, the height and setback regulations are part of

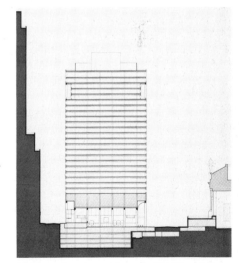

This section shows the relationship of the ground-floor spaces at Philip Morris to 42nd Street and Grand Central Terminal.

The Equitable Building by Ernest Graham which helped convince the public that some kind of control over building was needed in New York City. The Marine Midland and Chase Manhattan Bank towers that can be glimpsed at the left of the picture are taller, but occupy only 40 percent of their sites.

the most basic zoning controls, going back to New York City's (and the nation's) first zoning ordinance, passed in 1916. One of the buildings that helped persuade the public zoning was necessary was the Equitable Building (120 Broadway), finished in 1915 to the designs of Ernest R. Graham. This structure goes straight up from the building line for thirty-six floors and its bulk above the fifth floor covers 90 percent of the site. By the standards of the original zoning, Philip Morris has higher tower coverage and IBM and AT&T have taller walls going up from the building line than the Equitable Building. Minor infractions?

These seemingly technical changes mean big money for developers. The Greenwich Street regulations permit an increase in tower coverage from 40 to 55 percent, and assign a value to this change equal to a 20 percent increase in floor area. So you can see that going from 40 to 80 or 100 percent is a valuable benefit. In addition, these "minor" infractions are what permit the 499 Park and Philip Morris sites to be developed at all; otherwise the sites would have been too small for a modern office building. Those people who worry about midtown Manhattan being overbuilt should realize that these "minor" infractions have added to the developable sites and made the resulting buildings seem more bulky, as they occupy more of their site than any buildings constructed since zoning was enacted in 1916. A major change in zoning has been effected in the name of good design and small discretionary changes.

Despite all the reviews by Community Planning Boards and public hearings by the Planning Commission and the city legislature, it took a long time for the public, or citizens' "watchdog" groups, to understand what had been going on. I asked one of the architects whose building totally invaded the sky-exposure plane how the Community Planning Board had reacted to his proposal. His reply: "Oh, the building casts its shadow into another district, so they didn't care at all."

Once all the new towers were under construction, however, it began to be obvious that the city was approving some awfully large buildings. Critical newspaper articles appeared, and a coalition of civic organiza-

DESIGNING CITIES WITHOUT DESIGNING BUILDINGS

PROPOSED ZONING BULK (FAR) LIMITS

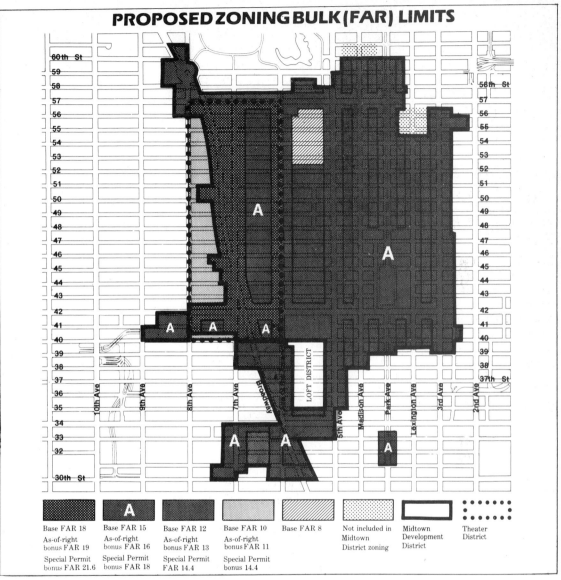

Base FAR 18	Base FAR 15 (A)	Base FAR 12 (A)	Base FAR 10	Base FAR 8	Not included in Midtown District zoning	Midtown Development District	Theater District
As-of-right bonus FAR 19	As-of-right bonus FAR 16	As-of-right bonus FAR 13	As-of-right bonus FAR 11				
Special Permit bonus FAR 21.6	Special Permit bonus FAR 18	Special Permit FAR 14.4	Special Permit bonus 14.4				

tions—including the Municipal Art Society, the New York Chapter of the American Institute of Architects, the Architectural League of New York, and the Parks Council—began urging that the city take a serious look at what it had been doing. The City Planning Commission undertook a two-year study of midtown Manhattan zoning. The working group was under the direction of Richard Bernstein, with Michael Parley as the principal urban designer. The commission went right on

The new midtown Manhattan zoning: the zoning densities show that the East Side has been rezoned, while zoning limits on the West Side have been increased in order to produce a more balanced development pattern.

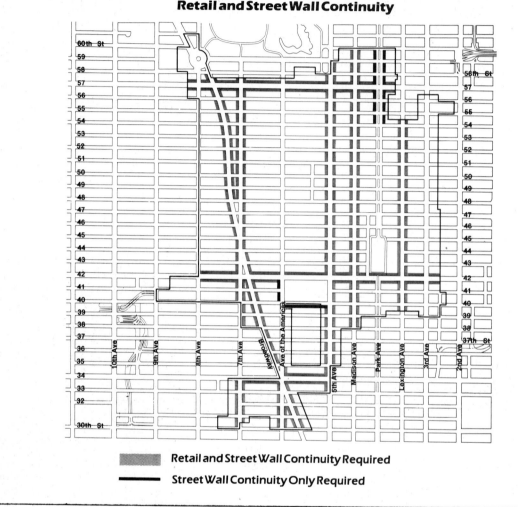

Retail and Street Wall Continuity

▨ Retail and Street Wall Continuity Required

▬ Street Wall Continuity Only Required

Above: the map shows places where the lower floors of the building must come out to the property line and where shop frontages must be provided to maintain retail continuity. All of midtown becomes a special zoning district. These provisions were developed under the direction of Richard Bernstein; the principal urban designer was Michael Parley.

passing special zoning provisions while the midtown study was in progress.

The result of the study was a group of comprehensive policies that dealt with the fundamental zoning issues of the midtown Manhattan business district. The avenue frontages on the East Side of midtown were designated as stabilization areas. The basic permitted building density was affirmed as a floor-area ratio of 15; but it was made more difficult to attain the additional 20 percent floor-area bonus that had been given for plazas and other amenities. The plaza bonus itself was reduced from a maximum addition to the floor-area ratio of 3 to a limit of 1. The mid-blocks on the East Side were actually downzoned to a floor-area ratio of 12. West of the Avenue of the Americas, midtown becomes a growth district, with the basic floor-area ratio on avenue sites increased to 18, with a potential, through bonuses, of 21.6 and a package of other policies designed to induce development. For the first time, New York City recognized that the policies for giving tax abatements should be coordinated with zoning, and tax-abatement possibilities are reduced on the East Side and enhanced on the West. In addition, specific areas, including the sites of the most significant existing legitimate theaters, are designated for preservation.

The new policies pick up the retail and street wall continuity provisions that had been important elements of the Fifth Avenue and Lincoln Square special zoning legislation and apply them to designated streets and avenues throughout the midtown office district.

Although the original intent of the Lincoln Square District was distorted when the Board of Zoning Appeals granted a developer more floor area than the district prescribed, and the architecture of the buildings is unnecessarily assertive, the arcade, the uniform cornice line, and the requirement that buildings come up to the property line on the Broadway frontage have all given the district a basic unity. The use-group provisions of the Lincoln Square District have been successful in ensuring appropriate occupants for the ground-floor shops.

The Fifth Avenue District had similar requirements that buildings hold the street line, although a setback was required only on the west side of the Avenue, and the legislation included analogous use-group and retail continuity provisions.

There have been three buildings constructed in accordance with the Fifth Avenue District provisions: Olympic Tower on the site of the Best & Co. store; the Piaget Building on the site of DePinna's; and the Trump Tower on the site of Bonwit Teller. Bonwit's is accommodated in the new structure—something that

Zoning requiring a uniform street wall and retail continuity was first used in the Lincoln Square Special District, which also mandates the arcade. The regulations produce unity, but they do not ensure architectural distinction.

Olympic Tower, designed by Skidmore Owings & Merrill, one of the mixed offices, shops, and residential buildings constructed under the provisions of the Fifth Avenue Special District.

Entrance to the experimental American Place Theater on West 46th Street, one of four new theaters constructed under the incentive provisions of the Special Theater District.

might well not have happened without the special district.

Evidently the original assumption behind the Fifth Avenue District, that the Avenue was vulnerable to redevelopment, was a correct one. A situation was foreseen and planned for; but none of the buildings constructed has completely lived up to the intentions of the district. The galleria space in Olympic Tower did not conform to the requirements of the zoning; the city has finally succeeded in getting it rebuilt by threatening to withdraw the building's certificate of occupancy. The Piaget Building has the correct massing and organization, but its public space also has not been completed to the specifications of the district, because the building was owned by the Pahlavi Foundation (controlled by the Iranian royal family) and has been beset by legal complications. The Trump Tower has turned out to be startlingly large, not just because of the special district, but also because of new zoning regulations that make it easier to amalgamate development rights from adjoining properties.

The city's new midtown policies remove the interior public space provision from the Fifth Avenue District and take away the additional 20 percent floor-area bonus, which was to be used for residential space. These changes reflect the evolution of a new political context for zoning decisions over the last decade. The interior public space provisions were in the district because the plaza, which the developer would otherwise have expected to provide for a 20 percent bonus, was in conflict with the retail continuity and hold-the-building-line requirements. The floor-area bonus for residential space was included to induce developers to continue providing space for department stores. Today, the city can simply mandate the building line and the stores, and reduce the total floor area that the developer can expect to build.

The Theater District will continue in force under the new midtown development policies. So far, this legislation has resulted in the construction of four new legitimate theaters: two large-scale musical comedy houses, and two smaller experimental playhouses. However, a

DESIGNING CITIES WITHOUT DESIGNING BUILDINGS

proposed new hotel on Times Square has threatened existing legitimate theaters, something the previous buildings constructed in the district did not do. The hotel complies with the district legislation in providing a new theater, but it also requires the demolition of the Morosco and Helen Hayes theaters, plus another theater building that has been used as a movie house for many years, and a smaller performance space, the Bijou Theater. Under the new midtown development policies, the significant existing theaters are designated for preservation. Up to a 20 percent floor-area increase can now also be earned by restoration of an existing theater or by the transfer of development rights from a designated theater structure. This improvement, which permits the preservation of the historic building fabric of the area and not just the function of the Theater District, is also a result of the changed political climate for zoning decisions, which permits far more emphasis on historic preservation than was possible in 1967, when the original Theater District legislation was passed.

The other major zoning changes initiated by the midtown development policies concern the bulk regulations: the provisions governing tower size and setbacks that have so often been the subject of negotiation and discretionary planning decisions. In midtown Manhattan at least, the Planning Commission is prepared to go back to a rule-book system where no negotiation would be either necessary or possible. The system is less restrictive than the regulations ostensibly on the books when all the special exceptions were being granted, but more stringent than many of the exceptions. The new rules are a return to a traditional zoning approach in which light and air for neighboring buildings were the primary factors, although the building line and retail continuity provisions prevent a return to the front-yard, side-yard mentality that characterized many of the buildings that took advantage of the plaza bonus. The combination of setbacks for light and air, plus walls that hold the building line, dictates an architecture of sculpted masses rather than the simple volumes the modernist aesthetic preferred. The 1916 zoning promoted an architecture shaped from the outside; the

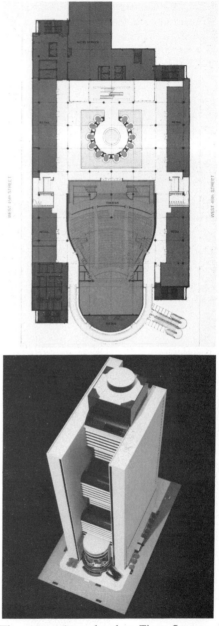

The proposed new hotel on Times Square, designed and developed by John Portman. The hotel will contain an excellent theater, but, for the first time, new construction in the theater district would result in the loss of significant existing theaters, the Helen Hayes and the Morosco.

Section through the Trump Tower, by Swanke, Hayden, Connell & Partners, Der Scutt partner in charge of design. Built under the Fifth Avenue Special Zoning District, the tower combines shops, apartments, and offices, and provides a covered pedestrian space instead of a plaza. The building's large external mass has been a subject of criticism, but most of the increase in size is the result of new rules facilitating the amalgamation of development rights from adjoining properties, not from bonuses in floor area achieved under the special district.

This series of illustrations (pages 113–115) from New York City's new midtown zoning proposals shows the development of tall buildings from the Equitable—which helped convince the public that zoning was needed—through the 1916 ordinance, the different aesthetic behind the 1961 zoning, and the new regulations.

1961 zoning followed modernist doctrine of the building as an isolated object, shaped by its internal functions; the new regulations are in some ways a return to the aesthetics of 1916. The regulations parallel changes that are going on within the practice of architecture. They are an expression of a "post-modernist" aesthetic —or at least the existence of post-modernism makes the acceptance of these new regulations possible.

The illustrations on the following pages describe this aesthetic journey there and back again. The last drawing shows the results of an alternative performance specification that may be adopted in preference to the ordinary rule book. Instead of conforming to a setback curve that relates the buildings to angles of visibility from the street, the building is measured according to the amount of "sky" left unobstructed. The method uses a daylight evaluation chart devised by consultants Kwartler/Jones–Davis Brody & Associates, which is derived from a device called a Waldram diagram (named for its inventor), which is a way of measuring daylight inside buildings. Development proposals that achieve appropriate scores on the daylight evaluation chart may be built even if they do not conform to the ordinary setback requirements.

There are other significant provisions in the new midtown zoning policies, including mapped locations where off-street subway entrances could be provided in new buildings and improvements in the requirements for plaza space. Presumably all of these new approaches will one day be applied to lower Manhattan and other areas of high-intensity development within New York City.

Before we conclude that the days of the one-sentence zoning resolution and the Negotiation Syndrome are gone forever, we should look at another important trend that has been taking place in New York City, where large-scale new developments have been turned over to the New York State Urban Development Corporation, which has the power to operate completely outside the framework of the city's zoning laws.

Battery Park City in lower Manhattan was covered by the complex special district provisions described in

DESIGNING CITIES WITHOUT DESIGNING BUILDINGS

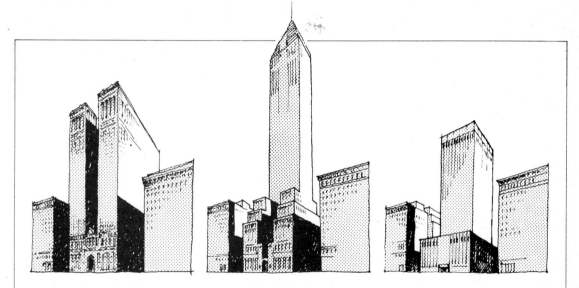

1. New York City's pioneering 1916 zoning resolution, the first in the nation, was in large part a response to such new buildings as the Equitable Building, 120 Broadway, which rose 540 feet straight up from its lot line without setback.

2. To protect the streets and avenues from being turned into dark canyons, the 1916 regulations established height districts. These limited the height a building could rise, in proportion to the width of the street it fronted on, until it had to set back. For each foot it set back it could rise "x" additional feet, the ratio depending on its height district. The two most commonly mapped height districts in Midtown had rise-to-setback ratios of 2½:1 and 3:1, equal to sky angle planes of 68.3° and 71.6° or an average of 70°. A tower rule permitted a portion of the building, up to 25 percent of the lot area, to rise without setbacks provided it was a distance from the street. There were no other limitations on height or bulk.

3. In reaction to the "wedding cake" shape of much of New York's skyline built to the 1916 zoning envelope, and to meet other needs, zoning was completely revised in 1961. A "sky exposure plane" replaced height districts to govern setbacks. To meet the need for larger office floors, the tower that could penetrate the plane was increased from 25 to 40 percent. A new tool to govern bulk was introduced, the floor area ratio (FAR). The basic floor area for the largest office building was set at 15 times the lot area, or FAR 15.

Note: dotted lines represent maximum zoning envelope

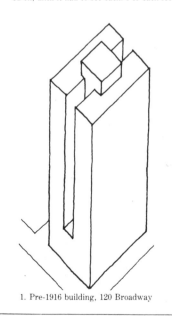

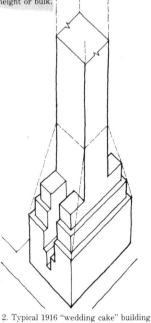

1. Pre-1916 building, 120 Broadway

2. Typical 1916 "wedding cake" building

3. 1961 tower on base, FAR 15

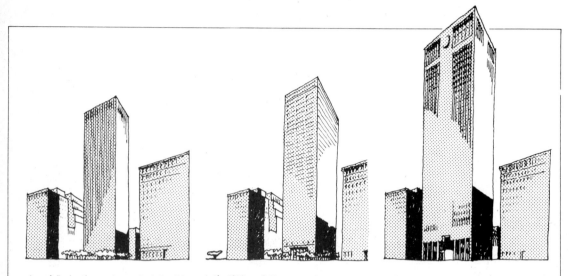

4. and 5. Another major goal of the 1961 zoning was to get more open space around new buildings. The "tower in a plaza" epitomized by the elegant new Seagram Building—actually a 25 percent tower conforming to the 1916 regulations—was the model. A 20 percent floor area bonus was offered to a building with a plaza, raising the largest building to FAR 18. It was the start of incentive zoning.

6. To meet other needs and to keep the continuity and vitality of avenues like Fifth and Madison from being destroyed by plazas, the incentive system was expanded. Bonuses were offered for interior spaces and sometimes compounded, bringing FAR up to 21.6. Combined with the restrictions of the tower regulations on the smaller lots left in the core area and the increasing use of "air rights," these interior bonuses put great pressure on regulations meant to protect the openness of the streets.

Note: dotted lines represent maximum zoning envelope

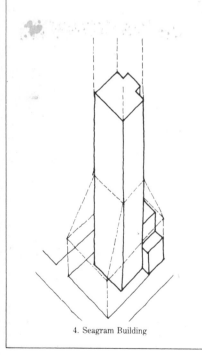

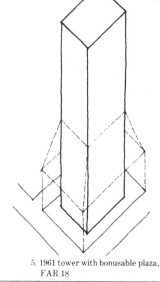

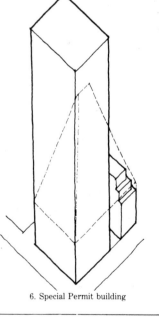

4. Seagram Building

5. 1961 tower with bonusable plaza, FAR 18

6. Special Permit building

DESIGNING CITIES WITHOUT DESIGNING BUILDINGS

7, 8 and 9. To return to zoning's basic principles, our architectural consultants examined how Midtown had developed under more than a half century of zoning. It is that actual development which defines the public expectation of daylight and helps set the standards for the new regulations. The 1916 and 1961 regulations recognized that the farther a building's mass sets back from the street the higher it can go; they allowed towers to pierce the sky exposure plane. But the plane and regulations still tended to prescribe a fixed building envelope. The new regulations are based on an actual standard of daylight and openness for the streets of Midtown, measured either against a daylight curve (first tier) or the percentage of unblocked sky (second tier). Both are derived from actual conditions resulting from Midtown's historic development. They give great flexibility in building design so long as the daylight standard is achieved.

Note: "daylight squares" in last drawing represent equal portions of the sky on the Daylight Evaluation Chart.

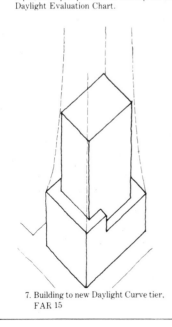

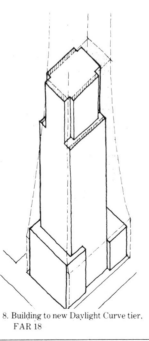

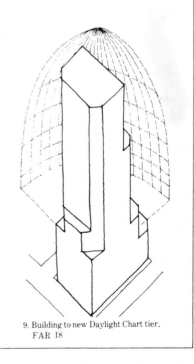

7. Building to new Daylight Curve tier, FAR 15

8. Building to new Daylight Curve tier, FAR 18

9. Building to new Daylight Chart tier, FAR 18

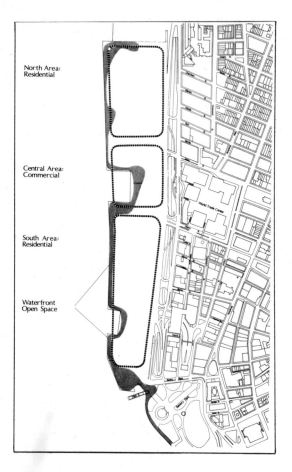
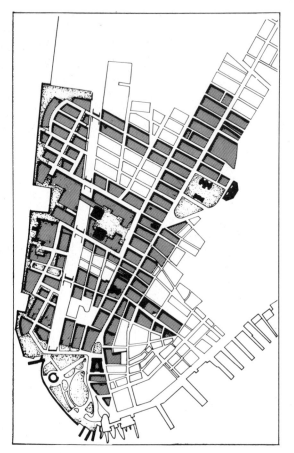

North Area:
Residential

Central Area:
Commercial

South Area:
Residential

Waterfront
Open Space

Drawings by Cooper-Eckstut Associates illustrating a revised plan for Battery Park City to replace the special zoning district shown in the previous chapter. Drawings from left to right show the land-use concept, design principles, special places, and the location of part space.

the previous chapter. The regulations were designed to permit the Battery Park City Authority to build without going back to the city for approval of each separate structure. At the same time, the zoning was meant to ensure the creation of an overall design concept, and the protection of the public interest in such aspects of the design as access to the waterfront, the preservation and definition of view corridors, pedestrian circulation, and so on.

For various reasons having little to do with zoning, not much progress in developing Battery Park City had taken place up to the fall of 1979. When the Battery Park City Authority was on the edge of default, the state legislature worked out a rescue plan, which included a provision that the Urban Development Corpo-

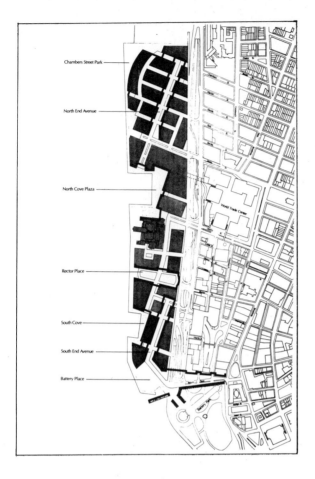
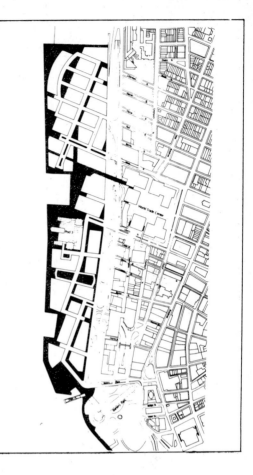

Chambers Street Park

North End Avenue

North Cove Plaza

World Trade Center

Rector Place

South Cove

South End Avenue

Battery Place

ration (UDC) condemn the land. The Battery Park City Authority would then lease the land from the UDC. As a result of this maneuver, the development now taking place at Battery Park City is not subject to zoning at all. The development controls are essentially a memorandum of agreement between the mayor and the governor, and are more a matter of courtesy to the city than a set of binding requirements, although individual projects will be reviewed administratively by the city to see if they are in "substantial" compliance with development controls. Later residential components will be subject to zoning analogous to that in other high-density residential districts of the city.

This process could be presented to the legislature as simple and uncomplicated, and may have been a factor

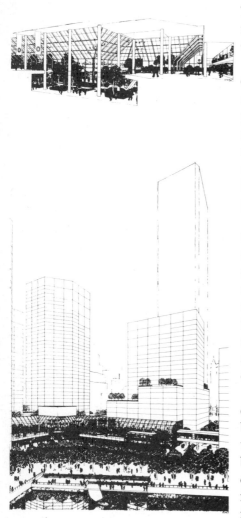

in the legislature's agreement to re-finance the bonds. The developer can also be assured freedom from Community Planning Board review, and from City Planning Commission and Board of Estimate approval.

The new development controls were prepared by the consulting urban design firm of Cooper-Eckstut Associates. Both Alexander Cooper and Stanton Eckstut had previously held directing roles in the city's Urban Design Group. They could have revised the existing special zoning district to meet changed development conditions. Instead, they went back to more traditional forms of control: planned development, street maps, parks, conventional plot-by-plot zoning.

The visual corridors that were an important part of the special district are preserved, but they take the form of traditional mapped streets. The complex esplanade controls, which permitted a mix of private development and public use, have been replaced by a simple park mapping for all the waterfront space. There is an illustrative site plan of a traditional kind, but it is legally a statement of intent, not a development control. There are illustrative perspectives, but they describe possible development rather than define it.

The new controls are thus a mixture of traditional development regulations of the type familiar to local builders, plus a traditional urban renewal plan where the buildings are specified in organization and mass before they have been designed. The innovative aspects of the special zoning district have been scrapped in favor of a conventional urban renewal approach. What is not as clear is whether the zoning methods were scrapped because they were unworkable, because they were perceived as unnecessarily complicated, or because the Urban Development Corporation preferred to leave itself as much freedom of action as possible. The adversary element of zoning is certainly removed when the development authority and the regulator are essentially the same entity. It is no longer necessary for the regulator to put cards on the table in advance.

Having secured its freedom from the city's legislative process, the Urban Development Corporation commissioned Cooper-Eckstut to produce a second stage of

Above: Cooper-Eckstut's development controls for the commercial core of Battery Park City use conventional urban renewal principles, complete with illustrative perspectives and opposite, an illustrative site plan that shows building shapes, elevator core locations, and other precise details before a developer has been selected or an architect chosen.

DESIGNING CITIES WITHOUT DESIGNING BUILDINGS

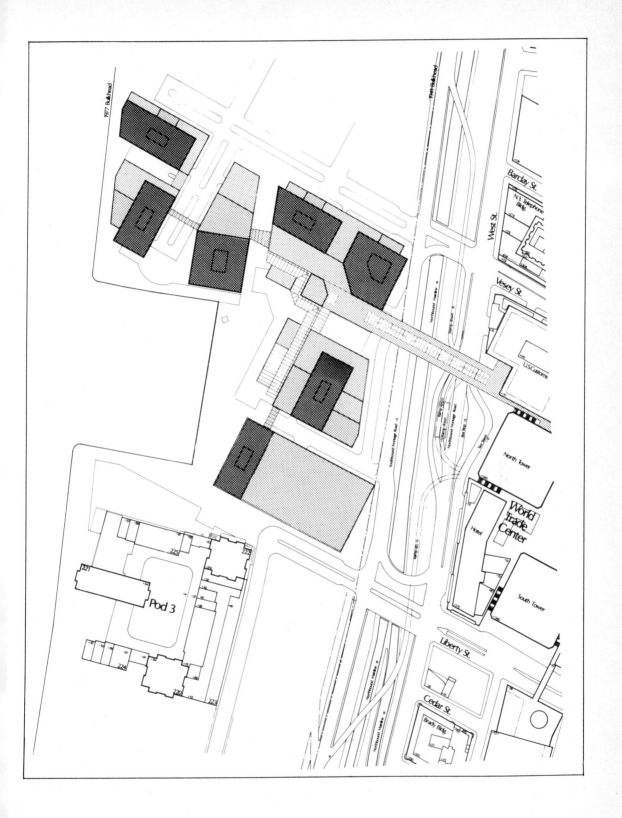

The actual design for the commercial core of Battery Park City. Cesar Pelli is the architect for Olympia & York Properties. Above: the whole complex as it will be seen from the Hudson River with the World Trade Center towers in the background. Below: the site plan; and opposite right: the entrance from Liberty Street. The architectural results are excellent, but the key to the success of this project is that it is all being designed and built at one time.

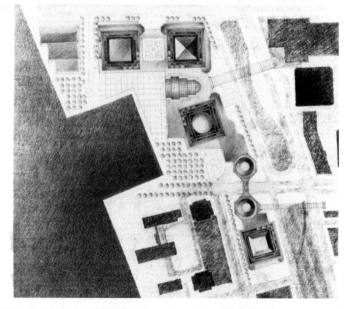

DESIGNING CITIES WITHOUT DESIGNING BUILDINGS

development controls that would give a more detailed set of requirements for the commercial core of Battery Park City.

What Cooper-Eckstut produced, and the UDC accepted, was a set of development controls that are far more detailed and explicit than anything that the city would have had the nerve to embody in a zoning district. The controls specify building locations, give specific configurations for public spaces, and even describe required external finishes.

The Urban Development Corporation then published these controls as part of a request for development proposals. The developer selected was Olympia & York Properties, which made its bid based on an intention to develop the entire commercial core. Olympia & York next held a limited architectural competition and selected a development scheme by Cesar Pelli & Associates. Pelli's design differs in subtle ways from the original Cooper-Eckstut concept, as can be seen by comparing the drawings illustrating the development controls with the plan and model photographs of the Pelli proposal. For example, Pelli has given the public galleria a new direction. Instead of being a space that parallels the riverfront, it becomes a space whose dominating motif is a connection to the river. This change is a matter of emphasis; it does not go against the original requirements. There are fewer office towers, and their floor sizes are larger, a change required by the developer; and Pelli has reconfigured the approach from Liberty Street by adding two small octagonal buildings, one on each side of the street. This device gives the site plan more unity than the Cooper-Eckstut proposal; in fact, the parcel south of Liberty Street had originally been designated as the site for a new American Stock Exchange building, and it had been added to the commercial core at the last moment.

A crucial factor in the success of the Battery Park City plan has been Olympia & York's willingness to develop the commercial core all at once. So many large-scale architectural plans have failed because they were carried out by different architects, for different clients, over a period of time long enough for development

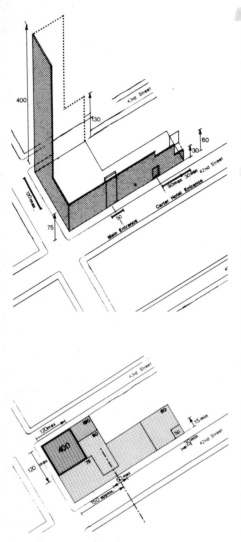

Diagrams by Cooper-Eckstut Associates of the development controls for the 42nd Street redevelopment project in midtown Manhattan. The controls include drawings like the one opposite which are almost as explicit as the schematic phase of an architect's design.

conditions to change. The Cooper-Eckstut plan was so explicitly architectural that it might well have met with the usual fate of urban renewal plans. Instead, it is likely to be the instrument of a great urban design success. But where the Cooper-Eckstut plan was good, the Pelli plan is better; partly because the architect was working with a real client and partly because Pelli is an exceptionally good architect.

The urban design controls for the 42nd Street redevelopment project in midtown Manhattan are an even more paradoxical combination of complete discretionary authority expressed as an explicit, and apparently unchangeable, series of building descriptions. The concept for redeveloping 42nd Street between Broadway and Eighth Avenue came originally from a study funded by a consortium of private organizations, including the Ford Foundation, with some support from the Port of New York Authority and the city government. The original plans were prepared by Richard Weinstein and Donald Elliott, with architecture and urban design by Davis Brody & Associates and Jaquelin T. Robertson.

The city decided to turn the implementation of this project over to the Urban Development Corporation, which retained Cooper-Eckstut to prepare the development controls. Cooper-Eckstut accepted most of the original design concept, but translated it into a series of explicit descriptions of building shapes, elevator cores, facing materials—in other words, almost to the level of detail that would be described in an architectural contract as the schematic phase of design.

The UDC's request for development proposals for 42nd Street explains that these development controls will take the place of the city's zoning ordinance for this project. These controls are the opposite of zoning, which seeks the general rather than the particular; and they turn away from the attempt to separate city design and building design, which was the principle behind the special urban design zoning districts.

Urban design controls in New York City seem to be evolving in two different directions. For smaller sites, in areas that are already substantially developed, the city

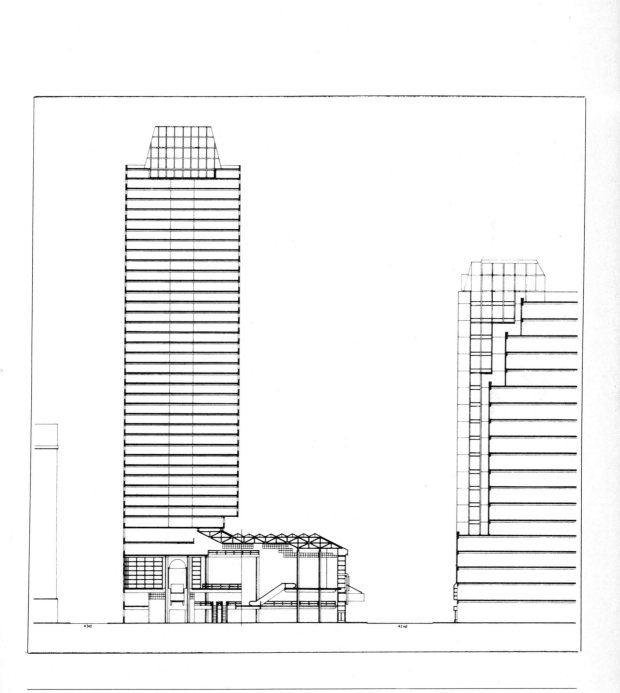

43rd   42nd

appears to be moving toward simpler, more uniform controls that extend some of the basic provisions of the original urban design districts over larger areas, while reducing the number of exceptions and special provisions.

In a landfill area like Battery Park City, however, and in urban renewal districts like 42nd Street between Broadway and Eighth Avenue, the tendency seems to be to take development out of zoning altogether through the agency of the New York State Urban Development Corporation. So far, the UDC has used its power to establish unusually detailed and strict design controls; but it has complete flexibility and could modify or remove these controls at any time.

Model of the original design concept for the 42nd Street redevelopment, made under the direction of Richard Weinstein and Donald Elliott, urban design by Davis Brody & Associates and Jaquelin T. Robertson.

8

The San Francisco Urban Design Plan

We must turn from New York to San Francisco to find a consistent set of zoning policies that are based on urban design considerations, rather than on individual special design districts, the more traditional forms of zoning controls, or explicit architectural requirements.

San Francisco has become a city where urban design is a major public issue. Most cities view their new downtown office buildings with pride, the signs of growth and progress. San Franciscans have learned to view new buildings with misgiving. Rightly liking their city the way it was, they have worried about the "Manhattanization" of their skyline.

The first public action reflecting this concern came in 1963, when the Board of Supervisors reduced the maximum permissible floor-area ratio in the downtown area from 25 to 20 on corner lots and from 20 to 16 on other sites.

In 1966, a new zoning ordinance was prepared that divided the downtown into four functional areas: a service district with a floor-area ratio of 7; a general district with a floor-area ratio of 10; a retail district that also had a floor-area ratio of 10; and a central office district with a floor-area ratio of 14. However, in all of these zones developers could attain a much higher density if they provided amenities that were rewarded with floor-area bonuses. These amenities included a plaza, which resembled the New York regulation except that

San Francisco's Incentive Zoning

the maximum bonus was 15 percent rather than 20. But where New York City's 1961 zoning had given bonuses only for plazas and arcades, San Francisco's 1966 ordinance had potential bonuses for a plaza and nine other building elements. These included two provisions relating to rapid transit, one to associated development for parking, three—besides the plaza—involving pedestrian access, two bonuses for bulk modification, and one for providing a public observation deck.

As the traditional reasons for restricting the size of buildings were to reduce congestion and the blockage of "light and air," the bonuses rewarded improvements in these functional areas. The highest-density district was mapped to coincide with the new BART rapid transit line that runs along Market Street. Direct connections to BART station mezzanines gained the highest bonus: up to 20 percent. A 10 percent bonus was also permitted if the building site itself was within a 750-foot walking distance of a transit mezzanine. A bonus was provided for directly accessible parking, which had, however, to be *outside* the highest-density zone. Up to a 15 percent bonus was given for sidewalk widening, kept distinct from plazas, which were defined as being at least 20 feet from the building line. There were also bonuses for side setbacks, and reduction of the tower size on higher floors—incentives to achieve results that were either mandatory or within the discretionary power of the Planning Commission in New York. The observation deck was a relatively small item, with a maximum bonus of 10,000 square feet.

When these provisions were adopted in 1966, they represented the most innovative land-use controls for an American downtown. They had nothing to say about the building's appearance, however, beyond some attempts to shape overall bulk. In the tradition of previous zoning they were functional, not aesthetic.

The new downtown zoning controls did not satisfy public opinion for very long. Three downtown projects in particular proved unpopular: the Embarcadero Center office buildings, the Bank of America Building, and the Transamerica Tower.

This photograph shows the buildings that caused San Franciscans to decide they needed a new method of controlling development. At right: the Bank of America Building, by Skidmore Owings & Merrill with Pietro Belluschi, a handsome structure by anyone's standards, but many San Franciscans considered it too big and too dark. At center: the serrated towers of Embarcadero Center, designed by John Portman. Despite the breakup of the building mass to diminish apparent size, and despite the fact that these towers are part of a publicly sponsored urban renewal project, people consider the buildings too large. At left are the Holiday Inn and the Transamerica Building; their shapes are considered too bizarre.

Embarcadero Center is part of a government-sponsored urban renewal project, so it clearly reflected public policy; but many people considered that its office buildings were too large and blocked traditional views of the water, despite the care taken by the renewal agency and the architect, John Portman, to keep the principal vistas open.

The Bank of America Building was designed by Pietro Belluschi and the San Francisco office of Skidmore Owings & Merrill. It is a skillfully planned building, whose restrained elegance and opulent materials would make it an ornament to almost any city. In San Francisco, however, it was seen as too bulky in relation to its height, and too dark, its brown granite at variance with the traditional light colors of the San Francisco skyline.

The Transamerica Building was the most controversial of all. It had been deliberately designed to call attention to itself, with its tapered profile reminiscent of an oil derrick. Public protests helped reduce the projected height to 800 feet, but it was still considered too tall and too bizarre in shape by a large number of articulate San Franciscans.

In addition to these prominent downtown buildings, a Holiday Inn on the edge of Chinatown and several new hilltop apartment houses in residential sections of San Francisco were also disliked by many people. The

A quotation and the illustrations from the "Fundamental Principles for City Pattern" section of the San Francisco Urban Design Plan. Principle number 2:

Street layouts and building forms which do not emphasize topography reduce the clarity of the city form and image. A: Tall, slender buildings at the tops of hills and low buildings on the slopes and in valleys accentuate the form of the hills.

B: Contour streets on hills align buildings to create a pattern of strong horizontal bands that conflict with the hill form.

old city was changing rapidly, and with each change there was more and more sentiment to conserve the qualities of San Francisco that everyone knew and loved.

In 1967, before the new incentive zoning provisions had come into use, the staff of the San Francisco City Planning Department had proposed an urban design plan for the entire city. After funds were secured, work began on this project at the end of 1968 and continued in stages until the completed plan was published in May of 1971. What had begun as an obscure staff project, unlikely to be published, much less to be turned into legislation, had become a hot public issue as the study progressed, because of public dissatisfaction with new development.

No one had prepared a design plan for an entire city since the days of the City Beautiful movement. Daniel Burnham himself had drawn a plan for San Francisco in 1904, just before the earthquake and great fire, but the document had been commissioned by a private group of civic leaders and was hardly a precedent. The planning department had to make up its methodology as it went along.

The story of the urban design plan has been told by Allan Jacobs, director of planning in San Francisco

DESIGNING CITIES WITHOUT DESIGNING BUILDINGS

from 1967 through 1974, in his frank and readable book *Making City Planning Work.* * Jacobs makes clear in his account that much of the initiative and the substantive work of this study came from young staff members trained as architects and urban designers. The project manager was Richard D. Hedman. There was also a citizens advisory committee to act as a sounding board. Eventually this committee was to play an important role in formulating the policies and principles of the plan, but Jacobs tells us that it took a long time before the committee began to function effectively; and Jacobs does not consider it to have been representative of constituencies as much as the judgment of its individual members. Other governmental agencies were invited to participate, but, according to Jacobs's account, their involvement was nominal.

It evidently took about a year for the participants in the study to work out a methodology and define what they were trying to accomplish. During this first year, the study produced three preliminary reports: *Background, Existing Plans and Policies,* and *Goals and Objectives.*

The turning point of the study came in 1970, with the completion of two important preliminary documents that were prepared with the assistance of outside con-

*American Society of Planning Officials, Chicago, 1978.

Another fundamental principle from the San Francisco Urban Design Plan, number 6: "When highly visible buildings are light in color, they reinforce the visual unity and special character of the city."

*Donald Appleyard, Kevin Lynch, and John R. Meyer, *The View from the Road.* Cambridge: M.I.T. Press, 1964.

sultants. These reports were an inventory of the city's *Existing Form and Image,* and a catalogue of *Design Principles.*

The concept of form and image owes much to Kevin Lynch, particularly to Lynch's book *The Image of the City.* Lynch's methodology combines the appreciation of form supplied by the professional with sociological questionnaires that seek to inventory public consciousness of city design. The link in this case was supplied by Donald Appleyard, who had worked with Lynch and collaborated on a book with him, *The View from the Road.* * Appleyard's particular interest in urban form as perceived through movement in vehicles was to skew the study to some extent. A subsection dealing with neighborhoods relates livability to an inverse ratio with through traffic (a perception arrived at through a study conducted with questionnaires). Much of the final document deals with devices for reducing through traffic in residential neighborhoods (see page 173).

The inventory of form—the result of work by the staff and by the consulting firm of Okamato/Liskamm —was comprehensive, stating on a block-by-block basis what, from an aesthetic point of view, was right and what was wrong with the city. It formed the basis for the most significant part of the urban design plan, the "Urban Design Principles," compiled by the staff, working with another consultant, Thomas R. Aidala. These principles were often subjective: "When highly visible buildings are light in color, they reinforce the visual unity and special character of the city." In the hands of the editor of the document, Peter Svirsky, the inventory and the principles, subjective as they may have been, became the basis for a clearly

DESIGNING CITIES WITHOUT DESIGNING BUILDINGS

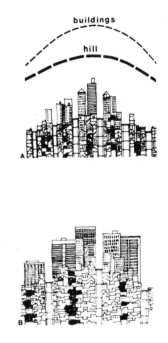

reasoned and consistent set of policies that could be used as the rationale for new land-use legislation.

It is this translation of subjective yet reasonable design judgments into an overall policy that is the key contribution of the San Francisco Urban Design Plan, and the reason why it should be studied with care. The sociological base, including the social reconnaisance survey by the consulting firm of Marshall Kaplan, Gans & Kahn, proved that the planners were interested in people as well as buildings and topography, and probably helped in the public hearing process; but the final document is essentially concerned with professional judgments of physical form.

The urban design plan included a set of height and bulk regulations that were to prove its most significant practical element.

The maximum height for buildings in different locations was determined from the overall formal analysis of the city rather than from the traditional rights of neighboring property owners or a more restricted district-by-district concept. A new means of controlling the bulk of the towers was also introduced. By setting the maximum diagonal dimension for towers in each district, the shape of the building on the skyline could also be controlled and not just the height.

The publication of the urban design plan coincided with efforts by a group headed by Alvin Duskin, then a San Francisco manufacturer, to bring about a much more drastic limitation on development through an initiative on the ballot. Duskin's approach had the merit of extreme simplicity. He proposed to set a limit of six stories on all new construction, period.

The fact that the campaign for the Duskin initiative

The first of the San Francisco Urban Design Plan's fundamental principles for new development:

The relationship of a building's size and shape to its visibility in the cityscape, to important natural features and to existing development determines whether it will have a pleasing or a disruptive effect on the image and character of the city. A: Tall, slender buildings near the crown of a hill emphasize the form of the hill and preserve views. B: Extremely massive buildings on or near hills can overwhelm the natural land forms, block views, and generally disrupt the character of the city.

The Duskin Initiative

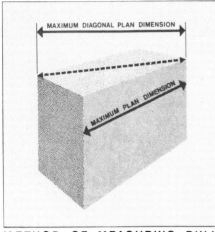

METHOD OF MEASURING BULK

MAXIMUM PLAN DIMENSION: The greatest horizontal dimension along any wall of the building, measured at a height corresponding to the prevailing height of other development in the area.

MAXIMUM DIAGONAL PLAN DIMENSION: The horizontal dimension between the two most separated points on the exterior of a building, measured at a height corresponding to the prevailing height of other development in the area.

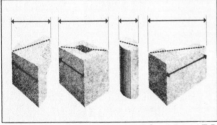

BULK MEASUREMENTS APPLIED TO OTHER BUILDING FORMS

One of the policies of the San Francisco Urban Design Plan is to relate the bulk of new buildings to the prevailing scale of existing development. The mechanism for doing this is to control a building's maximum plan and diagonal dimensions.

was going on at the same time that the urban design plan was completed was very helpful in getting the plan adopted. By comparison with Duskin's initiative, the planners' proposals struck the development community as positively moderate. At the same time, the planners were able to point out that six stories would be a substantial *increase* in permitted bulk for many of San Francisco's neighborhoods. The planners were thus in the happy position of seeming simultaneously more moderate about development controls, as far as the real estate business was concerned, and more conservative about new development in most neighborhood districts.

The San Francisco City Planning Commission formally adopted the urban design plan at the end of August 1971. The commission also passed a resolution to develop a new set of zoning controls that would help implement the plan. In the meantime, the height and bulk limits in the plan became a set of interim controls —overriding the existing, more permissive zoning. (The ability of the San Francisco Planning Commission to adopt interim controls is a useful means of staying abreast of events.)

The Duskin initiative went down to defeat in November, but received 30 percent of the vote, a very respectable showing for an urban design issue. Duskin and his supporters resolved to try again in June 1972, this time with a proposal that would recognize the difference between downtown and the neighborhoods. Heights of new buildings in residential areas would be limited to 40 feet; buildings downtown could be 160 feet—slightly more liberal than the original initiative. The second initiative still had the effect of raising heights in some neighborhoods where existing limits were 30 and 35 feet.

The hearings on the new city zoning proposals coincided with the campaign for the second Duskin initiative; and, again, the city benefited by appearing moderate in comparison to the initiative. The public interest generated by the initiative campaign also helped publicize the city's new zoning proposals and mobilize backing for them.

The urban design plan had shown a number of areas

DESIGNING CITIES WITHOUT DESIGNING BUILDINGS

These maps from the original urban design plan for San Francisco show the locations for height limitations and the different maximum plan and diagonal dimensions permitted in different districts. These regulations were made even more restrictive when they were actually enacted.

URBAN DESIGN GUIDELINES FOR HEIGHT OF BUILDINGS

URBAN DESIGN GUIDELINES FOR BULK OF BUILDINGS

in San Francisco besides downtown where the planners felt that tall buildings would continue to be acceptable, and some new areas for tall buildings as well. The effect of the public hearing process was to make the plan more conservative, with new tall buildings confined to the central part of the downtown. Even downtown, the plan was made more conservative; an absolute height limitation of 700 feet was placed on the highest-density area.

The second Duskin initiative received 43 percent of the vote on June 6, 1972; the San Francisco Board of Supervisors approved the new zoning regulations on July 31.

The Passage of the San Francisco Urban Design Plan

As Allan Jacobs points out in his book, for once the planning process worked as it was supposed to, with zoning proposals brought forward to implement a comprehensive plan. The height limitations, in the end, did not turn out to be markedly more subtle than the kind of limits proposed in the Duskin initiatives, but the bulk regulations have added another important element of control. The meticulous documentation of urban form provided the legal basis for the height limits and the new bulk controls, which had the effect of holding development substantially below the levels permitted by the other elements of the zoning, including the incentive provisions.

PROCESS FOR CONDITIONAL USES

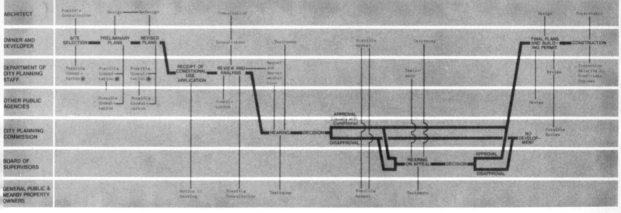

California's environmental quality legislation applies to privately funded projects as well as those that receive government support. Consequently, since the Environmental Quality legislation was passed in 1972, major new buildings require an Environmental Impact Review, and the Planning Department is the designated review agency. The urban design plan provides a conceptual framework for such a review, and the environmental legislation helps keep the plan in force. The Planning Commission is also using the approach process to make developers of office buildings create new housing in other districts of downtown San Francisco.

The urban design plan has not satisfied the no-growth advocates in San Francisco, who have again put much more sweeping height limits on the ballot as recently as the fall of 1979. There also continues to be dissatisfaction with the architectural character of new buildings constructed in the downtown business district. Richard Hedman, who had been the project manager of the original urban design plan, has described the architectural principles that the San Francisco City Planning Commission is now using in reviewing development proposals in order to avoid the deficiencies of many recent buildings.*

These principles include making new buildings come out to the property line on lower floors in order to

Approvals process under San Francisco's urban design regulations.

*"A Skyline Paved With Good Intentions," by Richard Hedman, in *Planning*, Vol. 47, no. 8 (August 1981).

reinforce the traditional street pattern, a requirement that these lower floors be "visually interesting," and that they relate to nearby buildings, architecturally and in defining street space. There are also new requirements to retain older buildings "or the significant portions of them" if they have architectural or urban design merit.

Hedman gives his first priority to a policy that would "Ban the box-top high-rise and approve only buildings thoughtfully shaped in relationship to their position on the skyline." He illustrates this point with a photograph of downtown San Francisco that shows how the 700-foot limit, passed as part of the urban design plan, has created a palisade of towers, all approximately the same height. It is not clear that reshaping the tops of these towers would really make much difference.

Hedman's real argument, however, is that the urban design plan needs to be reinforced by buildings that take account of their context. It is possible to define these contextual requirements, from the shape of the building on the skyline down to the position of the truck docks, and we will come back to these issues in Chapter 14.

9

Design Formulations
for Planned Communities

The concept of the planned community had a brief nationwide vogue in the United States during the early 1970s, in response to a now defunct federal program that provided low-interest, long-term loans for developing new towns. Unlike planned communities in Great Britain or Scandinavia, these HUD-sponsored new communities were not part of an interconnected series of national planning policies. Even in the countries that promote new towns as a policy, planned communities take a long time to pay off, with much money sunk into "front-end costs" for such items as roads and sewers, which don't return any income. In the United States, developers and government learned that planned communities often take too long to develop in terms of the competitive possibilities for real estate investment. At the present time, most new planned communities in the United States are resorts.

However, the planned community does represent the ultimate city design problem, in which the issue of designing cities without designing buildings is seen in its purest form.

The process of designing a new community is much more extended, and involves a great many more people, than the design of a building: but it goes through a recognizable series of stages, which are analogous to those of building design. As in the design of a building, it is possible to lose the ball game at any point. If the

A Four-Stage Design Process

site is badly chosen, or the program is wrong, the task is already hopeless. A good set of schematics is no guarantee that the concept will survive the design development process, and so on.

There seem to be four major stages in the design of a planned community. First is the site selection and programming phase, which involves the analysis of the land, and the selection—and testing—of some basic land organization principles. Next comes the land-use plan, which always embodies some kind of physical design concept. Such plans are sometimes called end-state plans, because they show the whole development at some indefinite time in the future. Frequently, however, the design principles upon which the land-use plan are based simply represent standard practice, and have little reference to the particular site and program. The third stage is the study of actual designs for infrastructure, lots and buildings, and the staging of the development process. Finally, stage four is the execution of the actual structures, at which point conventional architectural and engineering design contracts will be let.

It is evident that the skill with which these four stages of design are interrelated will have a significant effect on the quality of the ultimate result. There is often a big gap between stage two and stage three, while the developer waits to see if funding can be obtained or zoning and environmental approval received.

When it comes time to work out the actual staged development, the overall plan may turn out to be more of a statement of good intentions than a framework for what really happens. If there is a conflict between decisions taken in accordance with the overall plan—roads, for example—and the design of actual neighborhoods or centers, design quality is sure to suffer.

We will come back to this problem of interrelationships after we have looked in more detail at the individual stages of the design process.

The designer can play an important role in analyzing the site and in proposing organization concepts for the physical "infrastructure"—the roads, pathways, drainage systems, open-space networks, and so on—but is

A diagram of the McHargian process of analyzing ecological sensitivity to determine buildable sites, from the plan for Flower Mound New Town near Dallas, Texas, by Llewelyn-Davies Associates.

DESIGNING CITIES WITHOUT DESIGNING BUILDINGS

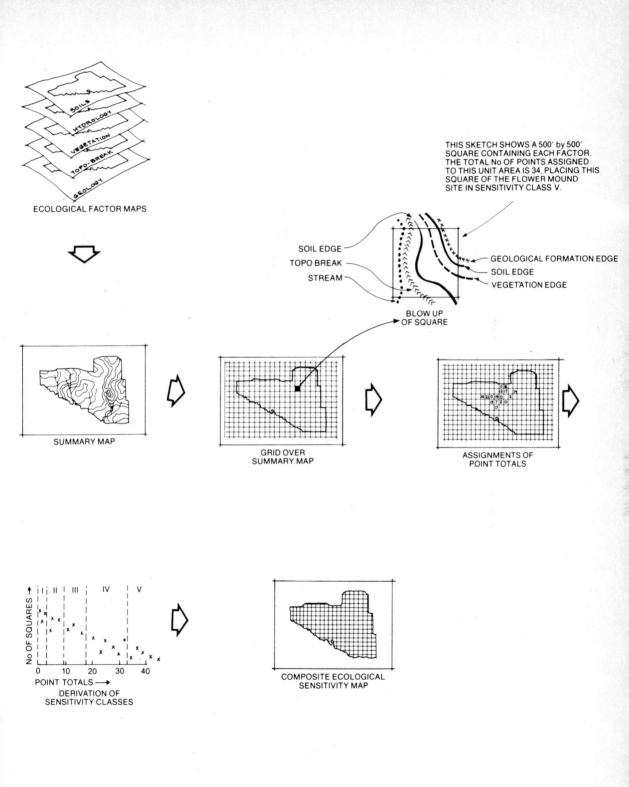

ECOLOGICAL FACTOR MAPS

THIS SKETCH SHOWS A 500' by 500'
SQUARE CONTAINING EACH FACTOR.
THE TOTAL No OF POINTS ASSIGNED
TO THIS UNIT AREA IS 34, PLACING THIS
SQUARE OF THE FLOWER MOUND
SITE IN SENSITIVITY CLASS V.

SOIL EDGE
TOPO BREAK
STREAM

GEOLOGICAL FORMATION EDGE
SOIL EDGE
VEGETATION EDGE

BLOW UP
OF SQUARE

SUMMARY MAP

GRID OVER
SUMMARY MAP

ASSIGNMENTS OF
POINT TOTALS

DERIVATION OF
SENSITIVITY CLASSES

No OF SQUARES
POINT TOTALS
0   10   20   30   40
II   III   IV   V

COMPOSITE ECOLOGICAL
SENSITIVITY MAP

Design Analysis of the Site

*New York: Natural History Press, 1969; pbk., Doubleday/Natural History Press, 1971.

not always consulted. Unfortunately, the designer frequently does not come into the process until the site has been selected and some basic developmental choices already made.

Sophisticated techniques for analyzing the ecology of a particular land development site are often associated with the name of Ian McHarg, a landscape architect and planner, formerly a partner in the Philadelphia firm of Wallace, McHarg, Roberts & Todd (later called WMRT, and now WRT). McHarg is the author of a book, *Design with Nature,* which sets out his basic theories. These seem so eminently sensible that it is hard to understand why they have not been accepted practice for many years.

Essentially, McHarg's point is that most site-planning techniques are devices for subduing nature. But because the site in its natural state embodies an equilibrium of complex natural forces, cutting down tree cover, bulldozing hillsides, or putting streams into culverts invites appropriate retribution: eroded topsoil, flooded basements, collapsed roads. In addition, there may be more far-reaching disturbance of the natural ecosystem: interference with bird migration patterns, climatological change, new vegetation patterns, changes in the water table.

McHarg suggests designing with nature, rather than against her, by analyzing the role played by each part of the site in the natural ecosystem and building only on land that can sustain development without far-reaching side effects. The diagrams on page 139 show a McHargian analysis done for Flower Mound New Town near Dallas, Texas, by another team of consultants that has accepted McHarg's premise. The drawing of vegetation on the opposite page was done by McHarg's firm to illustrate the natural systems prevailing on the site of the proposed Pontchartrain New Town, in New Orleans.

A preliminary ecological analysis can save a lot of trouble later. The proposed San Antonio Ranch new community in Texas received preliminary approval only to be tied up in litigation when people discovered

At right: a diagram by the firm with which Ian McHarg was then associated to illustrate the natural systems prevailing on the site of a proposed planned community near New Orleans.

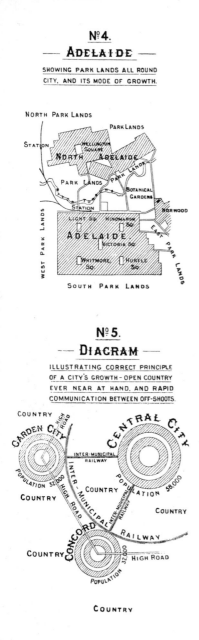

NORTH PARK LANDS

PARK LANDS

STATION

WELLINGTON
SQUARE

NORTH ADELAIDE

PARK LANDS

PARK LANDS

STATION

BOTANICAL
GARDENS

NORWOOD

WEST PARK LANDS

LIGHT SQ.   HINDMARSH SQ.

ADELAIDE

VICTORIA SQ.

WHITMORE SQ.   HURTLE SQ.

EAST PARK LANDS

SOUTH PARK LANDS

N⁰ 5.

— DIAGRAM —

ILLUSTRATING CORRECT PRINCIPLE
OF A CITY'S GROWTH - OPEN COUNTRY
EVER NEAR AT HAND, AND RAPID
COMMUNICATION BETWEEN OFF-SHOOTS.

COUNTRY

GARDEN CITY

HIGH ROAD

CENTRAL CITY

INTER-MUNICIPAL
RAILWAY

POPULATION 32,000

INTER-MUNICIPAL HIGH ROAD

COUNTRY

POPULATION 58,000

COUNTRY

COUNTRY

RAILWAY

CONCORD

POPULATION 32,000

COUNTRY

HIGH ROAD

POPULATION 32,000

COUNTRY

Diagrams from *Garden Cities of Tomorrow,* by Ebenezer Howard, showing how Colonel William Light's plan for Adelaide, Australia, influenced Howard in his formulation of the green-belt and satellite-city concepts.

that the town was situated in such a way that it would inevitably pollute the water supply for the entire city of San Antonio. One of the owners of the site was quoted in *Business Week* as saying: "Had I ever dreamed this project would turn into the nightmare it has become, I would never have thought about building a new town." Similar, if less drastic, experiences have happened at other planned communities.

Some of the basic organizational ideas for planned communities are so widely accepted that people have ceased to think of them as design solutions and have given them the status of basic assumptions.

The concept of the self-contained, planned community whose growth is held to an optimal size was put forward in 1898 by Ebenezer Howard, in a book entitled *Tomorrow: A Peaceful Path to Real Reform* (later retitled *Garden Cities of Tomorrow*). Howard was influenced in turn by various model company towns, and by the 1836 plan for Adelaide, Australia, by Colonel William Light. Light planned a belt of parkland all around the city of Adelaide, separating it from its suburbs, and particularly from the original planned suburb, North Adelaide, which was also surrounded with parkland.

Howard elaborated a theory of city design from the Adelaide example, giving us the principle of the green belt, an area of natural landscape that surrounds and separates communities. Other elements of today's planned community include naturalistic street and landscape design, the separation of streets and pedestrian parkways, and the concept of the neighborhood. Curving local streets and naturalistic landscape design in planned communities go back more than a century, to Frederick Law Olmsted's design for Riverside, Illinois, and before that to the curving paths and carefully contrived naturalism of English garden design. The cul-de-sac street and interlocking greenway pattern were used by Clarence Stein and Henry Wright at Radburn, a planned community in Fairlawn, New Jersey, more than half a century ago.

The concept of the neighborhood as the number of houses that represent the catchment area for an elemen-

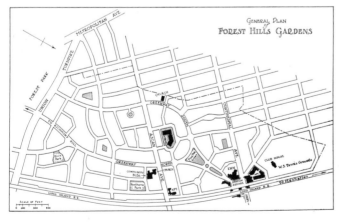

Above: the famous plan for Radburn, in Fairlawn, New Jersey, by Clarence Stein and Henry Wright, with its separation of pedestrian greenways from streets. Below: a diagrammatic plan of Forest Hills Gardens (designed by Grosvenor Atterbury and the firm of Olmsted & Olmsted), which influenced Clarence Perry in his formulation of the neighborhood concept.

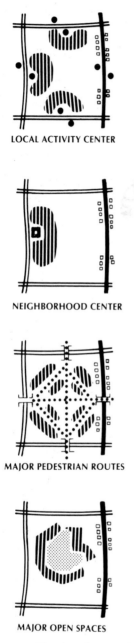

LOCAL ACTIVITY CENTER

NEIGHBORHOOD CENTER

MAJOR PEDESTRIAN ROUTES

MAJOR OPEN SPACES

These diagrams illustrate the organizing principle for planned communities developed by Llewelyn-Davies Associates. They come from that firm's plan for Audubon New Town, near Buffalo, New York.

tary school goes back to an essay by Clarence Perry published in the First Regional Plan for New York City, again more than half a century ago. Perry, in turn, was influenced by the design for Forest Hills Gardens, a planned suburb that had been begun in the early 1900s under the sponsorship of the Russell Sage Foundation.

Just because an idea has a long history is no reason to suppose that it is no longer valid, although in a period of accelerated social change, that suspicion does come to mind.

The late British planner Richard Llewelyn-Davies is known for questioning the relevance of neighborhoods in a planned community, and was also skeptical about the concept of a planned community as a self-contained entity with a green belt around it, believing that, in the age of the automobile, such isolation is not practicable. He preferred to think of a planned community as part of a larger network of relationships.

It is interesting that a form of cross-fertilization of rejected ideas is currently going on between Great Britain and the United States, with the Americans importing the self-contained new community out of dissatisfaction with formless urban growth, and the British looking to America for ways to loosen what is seen as overly rigid structure in their planned communities.

The pattern of organization suggested by Llewelyn-Davies is very much what you might see out the airplane window flying over any part of the American Midwest: the mile-square grid defining the landscape sector by sector. The illustrations on these pages show the Llewelyn-Davies formulation (originally worked out for the New Town of Milton Keynes in England) applied to Flower Mound New Town in Texas and Audubon New Town in New York State.

In the United States, it has become standard planning practice to design streets according to a hierarchy. The widest streets are the arterials, which connect major elements of the town or city. Collector streets are somewhat less wide, their function being to bring traffic from local, access streets to the arterials. Access streets need be only two lanes, might not require sidewalks or a hard edge. This street hierarchy is a reaction against

DESIGNING CITIES WITHOUT DESIGNING BUILDINGS

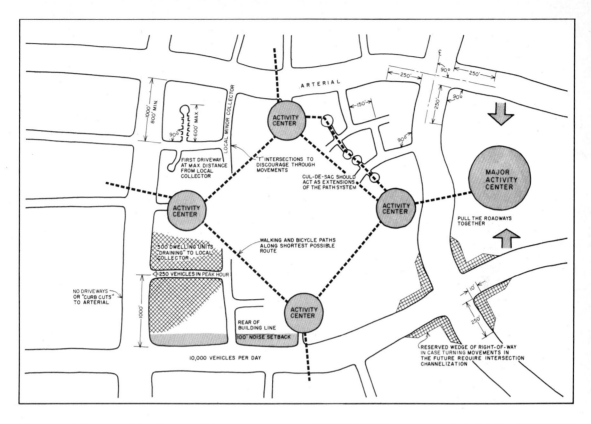

Above: an elaboration of the diagrams shown on the opposite page developed for the plan of Flower Mound New Town by R. H. Pratt Associates and Alan M. Voorhees & Associates from the basic theories of Richard Llewelyn-Davies. Right: Clarence Perry's diagram of a neighborhood, published in the First Regional Plan for New York City in 1926.

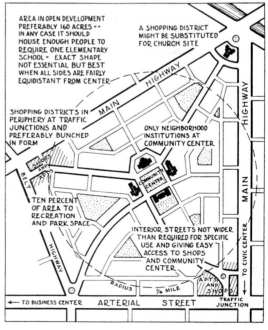

SERVICES DELIVERY CONCEPT
PONTCHARTRAIN

| REGIONALLY FO- CUSED SERVICES | COMMUNITY SERVICE SPINE | COMMUNITY SERVICE CENTER | COMMUNITY RETAIL CENTER | SPECIAL CENTER |

LOCATION MAP
PONTCHARTRAIN

| RESIDENTIAL DEVELOPMENT UNIT TYPE 1 | RESIDENTIAL DEVELOPMENT UNIT TYPE 2 | RESIDENTIAL DEVELOPMENT UNIT TYPE 3 |

These four maps illustrate the organization concepts for Pontchartrain New Town near New Orleans, designed by Wallace, McHarg, Roberts & Todd.

the uniform gridiron plan, in which any street was treated as a main street.

The Llewelyn-Davies formulation, by contrast, shows only two kinds of street: local and arterial. There is also a calculated ambiguity about the nature of the neighborhood, which might be within the mile-square grid or on either side of the arterial.

An inspection of the maps for the first phase development at Flower Mound indicates that Llewelyn-Davies may be making a distinction without a difference. There seems to be a strong similarity between the develop-

DESIGNING CITIES WITHOUT DESIGNING BUILDINGS

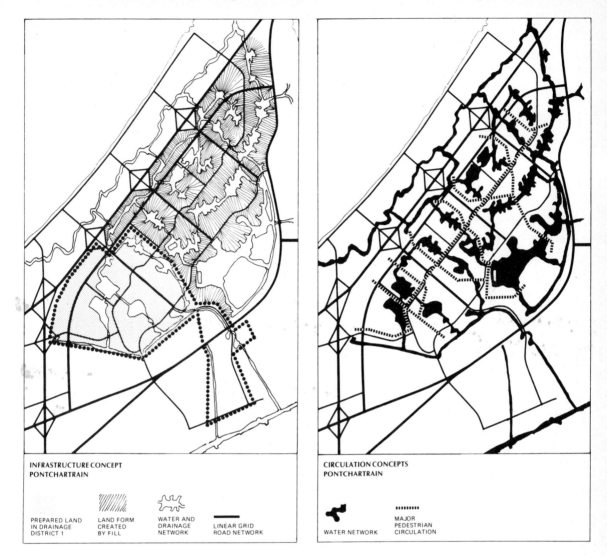

INFRASTRUCTURE CONCEPT
PONTCHARTRAIN

PREPARED LAND
IN DRAINAGE
DISTRICT 1

LAND FORM
CREATED
BY FILL

WATER AND
DRAINAGE
NETWORK

LINEAR GRID
ROAD NETWORK

CIRCULATION CONCEPTS
PONTCHARTRAIN

WATER NETWORK

MAJOR
PEDESTRIAN
CIRCULATION

ment at Flower Mound, planned without neighborhoods, and that at Reston, Columbia, and other communities, where the individual neighborhood was the basis for most planning decisions.

As a diagram, however, the Flower Mound or Audubon development pattern shows a much more modular distribution of major activities than has been usual in planned communities, with the mile-square pattern permitting greater flexibility of movement than is possible within a strongly defined street hierarchy.

The plans for Pontchartrain, a proposed new community on unbuilt land within the city of New Orleans, show the practical consequences of an extensive ecological analysis and a modular system of land-use organization.

The new town was to have been situated on 8,400 acres of what we used to call swamp, and have now learned to call wetlands, within a larger, 32,000-acre tract, part of which was to be preserved, and part of which would ultimately be developed as well.

Much of New Orleans has been built on land that was originally like this, and it is perfectly possible, through the use of drainage culverts and fill, to convert the landscape to buildable plots. However, this conventional engineering approach is completely destructive of the natural ecology of the area, and would have a bad effect on the surrounding wetlands.

What the consultants suggested instead was a natural drainage system, based on an interlocking network of canals and lagoons. By putting much of the open space on the site into waterways, the remaining land could be built up and contoured to drain naturally. Portions of the site could also be preserved in their natural state, and there would be a smooth transition to them.

The Pontchartrain plan used at a large scale a principle that has often been used in smaller development where the water table is high. In fact, there is a body of water, known as the real estate lake, that is often to be found around places like West Palm Beach and Fort Lauderdale, Florida. Although these lakes appear blue on maps, they are in reality often brown and cannot be used for recreation, as boat wakes, for example, would erode the banks.

What is interesting about Pontchartrain is the way in which drainage measures, plus three existing highway interchanges, were used to create a modular development concept that controlled the design of the whole community.

The relationship between stages two and three of the process of designing a planned community—that is, between the conceptual organization and the concepts for the actual physical development—is an extremely tricky one.

DESIGNING CITIES WITHOUT DESIGNING BUILDINGS

It is possible to go wrong by doing too much architectural design prematurely, basing a plan on housing types that turn out not to be marketable. It is also possible to go wrong by not doing enough architectural design, choosing a conceptual organization that does not work out well in the later stages. The most critical conceptual decision is the road layout. Many land planners develop the road organization for a planned community by going out and "walking the site," adjusting the roads not only to the contours but to the character of the land.

Other designers prefer a more assertive, man-made scheme of things. David Crane & Partners favor what Crane called the "8 vector grid," which was used for the town of Lysander being developed by the New York State Urban Development Corporation near Syracuse, New York.

Eight vectors means the four sides of a square and the four sides of the square formed by the diagonals of the original square. The site of Lysander is relatively flat, and strongly geometric man-made marks in the terrain are already present. The Crane design makes these into a systematic geometric pattern, which covers the whole area of the town. In addition, the town center is marked by another strongly geometric construction: a shopping complex, designed at right angles to form an "L," intersects with a sweeping quarter-circle curve, which is both a curving group of apartment buildings and a curve in a major roadway.

The designers of a planned community do not always have the opportunity to carry their ideas on to the implementation stage; nor does one firm of designers usually work out all the buildings in a planned community.

We are back to a familiar problem: how to design a community without designing all the buildings. One of the most ambitious attempts to answer this problem was the set of design controls worked out for Shahestan Pahlavi, a new center for Teheran, that was planned by Llewelyn-Davies International under the direction of Jaquelin Robertson. The association of this plan with the regime of the late Shah makes it unlikely that the

A Basic Organizing Concept for Planned Communities

proposal will be carried out in its original form. Nevertheless it is a document that deals in a very impressive way with the central issues of implementation.

Shahestan Pahlavi was planned for a 1,200-acre military reservation of largely vacant, hilly land that had been identified by the 1968 Teheran master plan as the site for a new city center, which would include government buildings, a major office and commercial concentration, and an embassy quarter, among other elements.

The expressway and rapid transit connections, the street system, and the location of development were all determined largely by the ridge and valley systems to be found on the site, with much of the lower-lying land being designated permanent open space.

The layout of the parks, transportation, and principal streets went a long way toward fixing the design, and, as much of the initial grading was completed before the Shah was overthrown, will influence whatever is done with the land in the future. The plan called for each of the principal streets to be landscaped in a distinctive way, with groves of trees and watercourses giving urban-design coherence even before the buildings were constructed.

The principal square was to have been surrounded with a "liner," patterned after a traditional arcade, which would present a uniform facade. The various buildings would then fit behind it. Other traditional devices for promoting design uniformity were also used, such as colonnades fronting on the boulevards and gallerias extending into the middle of the blocks.

The design controls were divided into mandatory requirements, discretionary guidelines, and illustrative designs. The mandatory elements were mostly traditional: floor-area limits, lists of permissible uses, and required parking ratios. The discretionary guidelines were similar in concept to the New York City special zoning districts, while the illustrative design model dealt with such issues as tower placements, location of subsidiary building masses and parking garages, design of landscaped spaces, and the organization of entrances to the transit system. It is not clear that this control system would have worked in Iran, where notions

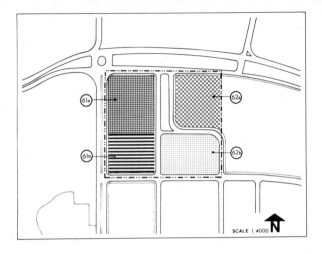

Left top: mandatory land-use controls for a development site at Shahestan Pahlavi. Left center: additional mandatory controls for the same site. The solid black lines are build-to planes, dashed line indicates an arcade. The dots define an area that is to be landscaped, and the diagonal lines define a visual corridor with a minimum width of 30 meters. The illustration at bottom left gives discretionary guidelines for such elements as bus and metro stop locations and preferred places for open space. Bottom right: an actual illustrative site plan.

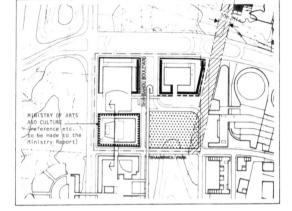

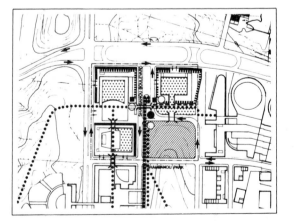

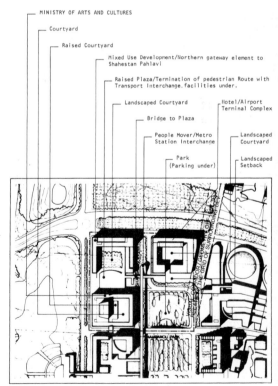

DEVELOPMENT AREA A

MINISTRY OF ARTS AND CULTURES

Courtyard

Raised Courtyard

Mixed Use Development/Northern gateway element to Shahestan Pahlavi

Raised Plaza/Termination of pedestrian Route with Transport interchange facilities under.

Landscaped Courtyard

Hotel/Airport Terminal Complex

Bridge to Plaza

People Mover/Metro Station Interchange

Landscaped Courtyard

Park (Parking under)

Landscaped Setback

Design Controls for Subdivision Development

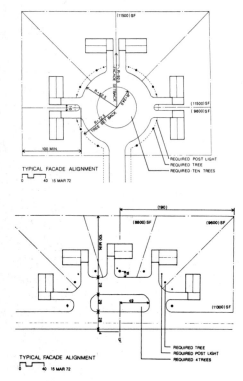

TYPICAL FACADE ALIGNMENT

TYPICAL FACADE ALIGNMENT

Two examples of design standards for subdivision developers drawn by David Crane & Partners for Flower Mound New Town, near Dallas, Texas.

about agreements and negotiation seem to be different from Western concepts, but it makes a great deal of sense. Architectural design is included as part of the development control system, but illustrates the more general performance standards that are the actual requirements. The public investments in parks and streets are also a major element of the design controls, and the fact that much of the plan was for government buildings would also have helped to fix the design.

The development controls developed for Lysander and Flower Mound by David Crane & Partners follow a somewhat similar method, although at a much lower density and more relaxed rural scale. The typical sections through roads and pathways, shown at left, are developed with the engineers and landscape architects as definitive design standards.

The sub-division controls for Flower Mound use methods that also have a lot in common with New York City special zoning districts. The designer has created "build-to" lines, specified some elements of building location, and set landscaping standards. Nothing is said, however, about whether the house has shutters or diamond-paned windows. The pressure to get some income flowing to offset the extraordinary front-end costs of planned communities in turn creates pressures to stop back-seat-driving builders. These controls have the advantage of being explicit, relatively objective, and easily understood and agreed to in advance.

As we move on into an era of relative scarcity of natural resources, conservation and the effective management of land will become more and more important. We can expect that there will be more regional and statewide planning, and more zoning regulations that are related to environmental considerations. It is logical to anticipate that new development will make more use of urban and environmental design, and that these design control methods will be developed further. In this way, more and more communities will become planned communities.

DESIGNING CITIES WITHOUT DESIGNING BUILDINGS

PART THREE

THE ELEMENTS OF A DESIGN AND DEVELOPMENT STRATEGY

10

Land-Use Strategies

Because we are coming to value continuity with the past more than novelty, balance with nature more than a controlled environment, and stability more than constant change, we are experiencing a fundamental transformation in the way that land-use policies are created and administered. The zoning ordinance has been the most significant method of controlling land use, even when land-use policy was really made through exceptions to zoning, rather than by following the map and text. The basis of zoning is the separation of land uses, which has prevented you from suddenly finding an office building or a factory next to your house, although you might have to drive several miles to buy the Sunday paper or a few groceries.

The doctrine of separation implied that everything within a given district would ultimately be built or rebuilt. If an area was zoned for tall office buildings, an old theater or railway station that happened to be in the way would ultimately be replaced. If a bucolic landscape was covered with neat rectangles on the zoning map, it would ultimately become houses or factories, regardless of its scenic or ecological value.

But we don't wish to build everywhere, or to build everything new. We have come to value historic preservation, and to seek the re-use of old buildings, which may be in the wrong zone for their new use. We have discovered that we should not promote the kind of real

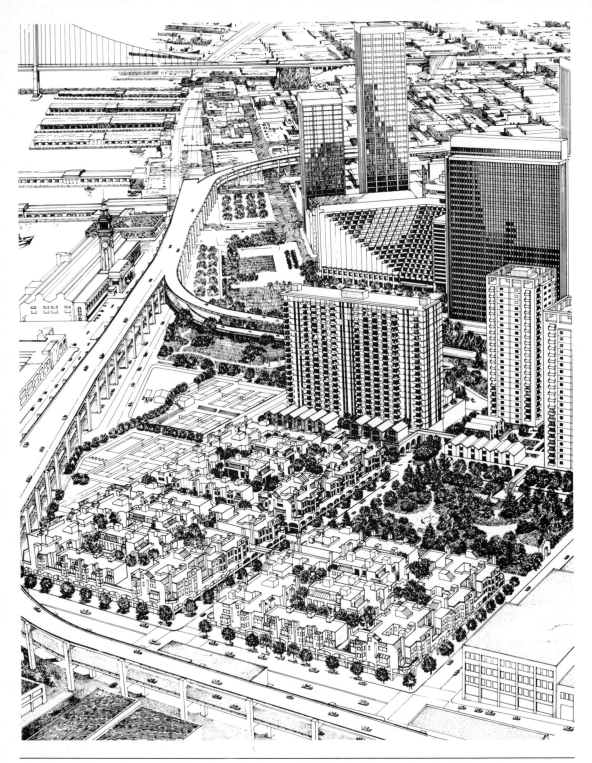

THE ELEMENTS OF A DESIGN AND DEVELOPMENT STRATEGY

estate development that takes unbuilt land and attempts to fulfill the biblical prediction that "Every valley shall be exalted, and every high place made low." Certain parts of the landscape ought not to be built upon at all, no matter what their current zoning, and the rest should be developed in a way that blends with natural contours and fits into existing microclimates. At the same time, land-use regulation should promote the preservation and adaptive re-use of valuable old buildings; it shouldn't work against it.

Our realization of the scarcity of energy resources is also modifying our assumption that the separation of land uses is desirable. We need opportunities to walk or bicycle to our destinations, and land uses have to be related more closely to transportation corridors. Paradoxically, the technologies of artificial light and ventilation have improved greatly since zoning was first invented, so that when we do choose to use scarce energy resources to create an artificial climate, we can now combine different uses in a single building far more easily than in the past.

Ultimately we will change our land-use regulations to take account of these new realities; but changing the rules will be complicated. Environmental zoning implies regional or statewide planning, with attendant controversies about home rule and local autonomy. Zoning landmark buildings to help preserve them may well be constitutional; the Supreme Court in its opinion on the Grand Central Station case stated that landmark designation, if conducted comprehensively, was itself a comprehensive plan. One of the major tests of the legality of zoning has been whether it embodies a comprehensive plan. Historic districts have become an accepted part of land-use control, but remapping individual landmark buildings to reduce their redevelopment potential without making it possible to transfer their development rights is still an untested zoning technique.

We are also far less willing to leave the initiation of development to the private real estate market than was the case when zoning regulations were first enacted. Localities now use a variety of development incentives:

This drawing shows the complete transformation of land uses in downtown San Francisco through government intervention. In the background at right are the office buildings and hotel of the Embarcadero Center project; in the middle ground, the towers and townhouses of the Golden Gateway project; and, in the foreground, the townhouses of the most recent part of Golden Gateway. The parks and tennis courts are also new. In the lower right-hand corner is an older loft building, representative of the structures that once characterized the area.

Above: a dramatic view of the townhouses at Golden Gateway from the podium level.

Opposite top: in the newest part of the Golden Gateway development, shops and offices surround the parking structure that provides a podium for the townhouses. In older parts of this project, there is only a garage at street level, so that the street level is a continuous dead wall.

The section opposite below shows the relationship of houses to parking, stores, and offices. Architects are Fisher-Friedman Associates.

land assemblage, land subsidies or "write-down" after land has been assembled, interest subsidies, tax abatements, direct grants from Federal Community Development funds or from Urban Development Action Grants (the ubiquitous "UDAGs"). These actions are part of land-use policy, although they are not always thought of in this way.

Localities thus need a land-use strategy that takes into account preservation and environmental objectives that may not be embodied in zoning, and that seeks to modify the workings of the real estate market by protecting existing uses that are considered valuable, and encouraging new uses that would not otherwise be developed.

Most places have an implicit land-use strategy, several political objectives that are generally accepted. In Pittsburgh, the mayor has been able to articulate his policy objectives in three words: "jobs and housing." It is city policy to promote the development of new jobs and to improve housing conditions and the quality of life in residential neighborhoods. In another locality, say, a suburb full of large houses, the policy might be to preserve the residential atmosphere but to improve the tax base by permitting a few corporate headquarters or a district of "clean" industry.

In order to have a successful land-use strategy it is necessary to have a more sophisticated understanding of the real estate market than has been traditional in government agencies. The local government may also find itself in the political position more usually occupied by real estate developers. In Charleston, South Carolina, for example, there may have been consensus that land-use policy should both seek to strengthen the economic base of the central city and enhance the livability of the central area, but in the case of a proposal to build a convention hotel and meeting rooms there was a perceived conflict between these two objectives.

The result is that localities are forced to think in strategic terms, to understand the interconnections among issues, and to accept that, while objectives may remain constant, tactics may have to be adjusted over

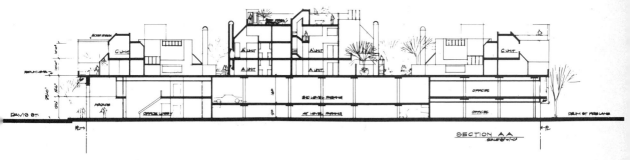

SECTION AA

time. Instead of traditional land-use planning, localities must have a land-use strategy.

If the strategic objective is to preserve downtown retailing, more than traditional parking and beautification programs may be required. It may be necessary to stop facilitating the construction of shopping centers in outlying regions. If a proposed shopping center is in a suburb beyond the city limits, it may be necessary to engage in legal tactics, such as seeking to prevent any government subsidy in the construction of the center.

If the strategic objective is to promote middle- and upper-income housing downtown, economic incentives are clearly going to be important; but, again, it may make sense to consider closing off some of the potential alternative locations for such housing.

It will become increasingly common to find conflicts in strategic objectives as localities continue interventionist policies. Expanding the space available to an older industry to keep it within the city limits may require the removal of nearby houses. When this happens through private real estate transactions, it is not a public issue. However, if a city assembles the industrial land through urban renewal, the conflict becomes a matter of public policy. In some cases there may not be a resolution that satisfies everyone; in others, it may

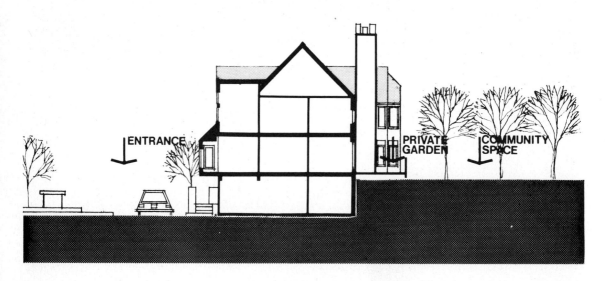

ELEMENTS OF A DESIGN AND DEVELOPMENT STRATEGY

be possible to promote a land-use strategy that satisfies multiple objectives. For example, it is becoming increasingly usual for localities to require that office buildings constructed within a retail district provide shops on the lower floors and preserve the retail continuity of shopping streets. A plaza is not what you need at an important retail corner, particularly if the frontage on the plaza is occupied by a bank. A policy of avoiding such plazas makes economic sense for the building owner, although it may not evoke the same connotations of prestige as a plaza. Where land-use strategies run counter to the owner's immediate economic advantage, incentives may have to be found. The Theater District in New York City, described in Chapter 6, is an early example of this type of land-use strategy.

The adoption of an interventionsist land-use strategy renders many traditional zoning and planning practices obsolete. If the historical absorption rate for new office space in a city center has been 300,000 square feet per year, and if the city is actively seeking to preserve downtown retailing and promote downtown housing, it no longer makes very much sense to leave 100 or so acres of prime downtown land zoned for the highest office building density. That beautifully illustrated consulting study that shows both banks of the river lined by some 10,000 units of apartments doesn't provide much of a guide to public policy if the historic absorption rate for upper-income apartments has been 150 units a year. The old brick warehouses, designed for industries that no longer exist, are on the National Register of Historic Places. They are also empty. Time to change the zoning map.

Land-use planning must now take into account preservation and ecological objectives, and must relate to land-use strategies that deal with economic, political, and social feasibility. The traditional separation of land uses must give way to new types of mixed-use districts, which will encourage retailing in office buildings, for example, or manage the transition from industrial to residential use.

Opposite: section through new private townhouse along the Loring Park Extension in downtown Minneapolis shows how security for each house is maintained by separating the street from a private, garden level for the residents. The photograph, below, shows some of the houses. Creating new, downtown housing is an important land-use objective in many cities and security is one of the issues that must be addressed. Architects are Frederick Bentz/Milo Thompson & Associates, Inc.

A map showing the boulevards and parks constructed while Baron Haussmann was Prefect of the Seine during the regime of Napoleon III. Black lines leading into the center of Paris are railroads; note how many of the boulevards connect railway stations to central destinations.

11

A Public Open-Space Policy

Any discussion of public open-space policy today must begin with the work of Baron Georges-Eugène Haussmann, Prefect of the Seine from 1852 to 1869 during the Second Empire, the reign of Napoleon III. The transformation of Paris during those years often gets a bad press. Because it was Louis Napoleon himself who had given Haussmann a rough layout of the new boulevards he wanted, as well as the location of major parks, critics often assume that the transformation of Paris was directed toward achieving dictatorial or military ends. What are the boulevards except a device to rush troops from one quarter of the city to the other, and keep the citizens from erecting barricades? Paris, to these critics, was treated like a hunting forest for a baroque royal court, with *allés* cut through the trees to permit the formal progress of the hunt. There is an element of truth in this analysis, and the *allé* is one of the ancestors of the boulevard. But anyone who looks at a map can see that the major purpose of the Parisian boulevards was to help everyday traffic get from one part of the city to another. The boulevards connect the railway stations, which in the 1850s had just been constructed, with the major central destinations of the old city. The design of the elegant tree-lined boulevards also goes far beyond the requirements of military expediency. While Haussmann and his associates did not invent any of the elements they used, they put them together in a defini-

A Parisian boulevard around 1890, showing the uniform cornice line imposed by the maximum height that people will walk upstairs.

A detail from Burnham's plan for Chicago of 1909 showing the buildings that would be grouped around the proposed Civic Center. Burnham tried to apply the Parisian uniform cornice line to elevator buildings, choosing approximately 14 stories as the limit. There was no legal or economic enforcement for this concept, however, and it didn't work. But it has worked in Washington, D.C., where there is a legal height limit.

Haussmann: Paris Transformed. New York: Braziller, 1971.

tive way that has been vastly influential, and indeed still influences us today.

It has also become fashionable to criticize Haussmann for destroying the old Paris; but as Howard Saalman points out in his excellent essay,* it is really remarkable how much of the old Paris has remained, considering the scope of the changes Haussmann initiated. Compared to changes proposed later by Eugène Henard or Le Corbusier, or the standard practice of urban renewal in the United States during the 1950s and 1960s, Haussmann's measures were highly selective.

Haussmann has left us a new image of the city that has been used in Europe from Helsinki to Barcelona, and in the United States was an important element in the City Beautiful movement, which swept the country after the World's Columbian Exposition of 1892–1893. The image itself was not militaristic or dictatorial, but there is no question that Haussmann's means of implementation required the use of a powerful dictatorship. We are left with a paradox: we admire the continuity of Paris, the unbroken sweep of the boulevards, the symmetry of the public squares, the way these squares and boulevards focus attention on important public buildings. But we are not prepared to hand over almost all new construction to a public authority with sweeping powers of condemnation. There are elements

ELEMENTS OF A DESIGN AND DEVELOPMENT STRATEGY

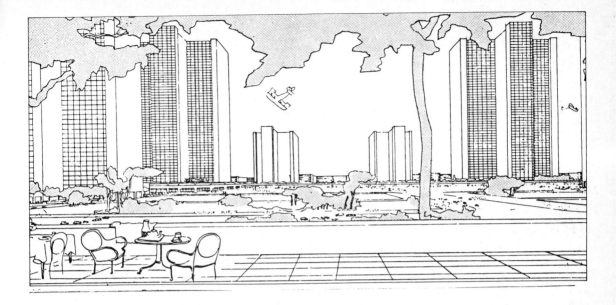

of Haussmann's Paris in almost every American city: tree-lined boulevards, large parks with the winding paths of the English garden, public buildings in the French Academic style. These Parisian touches were all financed by local governments, and their limited scope reflects the limits of governmental authority. As we saw in Chapter 5, when it came to implementing those aspects of Burnham's Haussmannesque Chicago Plan of 1909 that applied to the private real estate market, there was no consensus about how to do it; and these privately financed components were thus never completed, although many of the public elements were.

When we talk about public open space today, we also have to consider another vision of Paris, Le Corbusier's Voisin Plan of 1922. Corbusier's vision of the tower in a park, while destructive of traditional cities, deals with an element that Haussmann did not take into account, the tall office building, which began to be developed just as Haussmann's reign was coming to an end. For a while the fashion for towers in parks swept the world much as Haussmann's boulevard concept had done. Now that we have had some experience with cities of towers, we realize that the continuity of street frontage is an important design element of cities. We need to

Le Corbusier's 1922 drawing shows a better appreciation of the tall building's potential height and form, and its compensating need for open space. Note how much the coherence of Le Corbusier's design depends upon uniform height and building form. Without strong government regulations (sometimes found in authoritarian socialist countries), this concept doesn't work. The coherence of the street front is lost, and nothing new takes its place.

The Burdick Street Mall in downtown Kalamazoo, Michigan, proposed in Victor Gruen's *1980 Plan* of 1958, was the first downtown pedestrian mall to be created in the United States. This photograph was taken just after completion.

invent a new image, however, one that combines the continuity of Haussmann's pre-elevator structures with the permanent reality of the tall office building, hotel, and apartment house.

Walking in Paris not long ago, I was suddenly struck by a revelation both profound and obvious: no parking lots. One of the great virtues of the Parisian streetscape, going beyond uniform cornice lines, street trees, and the geometries of axial planning, is that almost every building lot is occupied. When you compare central Paris to the typical American downtown, the difference is obvious. In the United States, except for the biggest and most densely developed city centers, or along the most important streets, every other block seems to be a parking lot. The economics of parking are often more attractive than operating a building in the same location. Consider a parking lot in a small city downtown. Let us imagine the operator collects $3.00 a space for all-day parking, 250 days a year. A parking space repre-

     ELEMENTS OF A DESIGN AND DEVELOPMENT STRATEGY

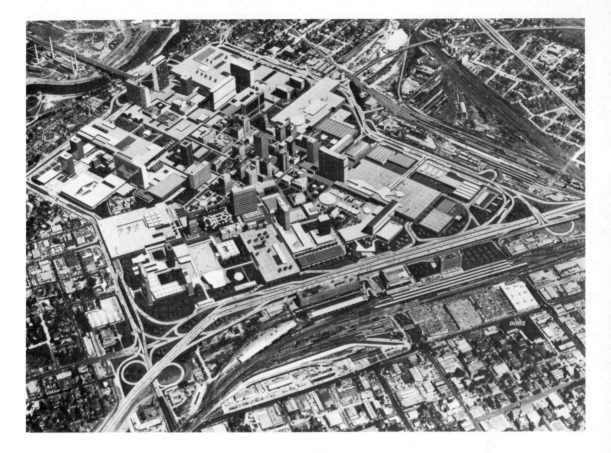

sents perhaps 300 square feet, so that the annual rental measured in dollars per square foot is something like $2.50. There are no taxes on a building, only on the land; the operating costs are minimal; the capital costs practically nonexistent. Compared to paying taxes, heating, and other operating costs for a partially occupied building, parking is a most attractive option. No public open-space policy for any city will be truly successful until it deals with the pervasive reality of parking lots. We need to invent interim uses for land that are as economically attractive as parking; we need parking policies (see Chapter 13) that deal with parking on a more definitive basis; and we need to take governmental measures to preserve buildings and make tearing them down for parking lots less attractive to owners. A higher tax on downtown vacant land would do it. If we

Aerial perspective of Victor Gruen's 1956 plan for the revitalization of downtown Fort Worth, Texas. An expressway loop around the city center gives access to garages, which are within a few minutes walk of the pedestrian precinct, created by closing the streets of the central business area. This proposal was never implemented in Fort Worth but has proved a very influential concept as a means for helping downtowns compete with suburban shopping centers. Gruen himself was able to realize a somewhat more modest version of the scheme for downtown Fresno, California, in 1964. In the many other cities where downtown malls have been created, the importance of parking and expressway access has sometimes been forgotten.

The Importance of Streets as the Public Open-Space Armature

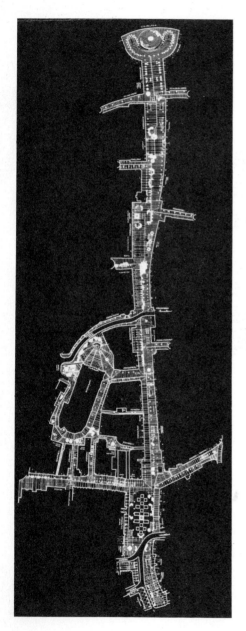

can't beat parking lots, we ought to find ways to screen them, through landscaping or even by permanent structures.

A second element basic to any public open-space plan is to recognize the importance of streets as the framework of public open space. Such recognition does not imply a return to Baron Haussmann or the City Beautiful movement, but an understanding that the streets are the only constant factor in cities where development takes place in an incremental manner in response to a private real estate market.

There is much that can be done to improve the environment of the street itself. We are beginning to have a body of experience in the creation of pedestrian malls and transitways from streets, especially in downtown retailing districts. The first such mall in the United States was constructed on Burdick Street in downtown Kalamazoo, Michigan, according to a plan by Victor Gruen & Associates that was completed in 1958. The Kalamazoo plan embodied elements of Gruen's famous 1956 plan for Fort Worth, which separated automobiles and pedestrians in a comprehensive way but has never been carried out. The Fort Worth plan, in turn, derived from European projects implemented just after World War II, such as the Sergelgatan in Stockholm and the Lijnbaan in Rotterdam. Another influential European development was the closing of Copenhagen's main shopping street, the Strøget, to automobiles in 1962. The Copenhagen plan had the merit of simplicity of execution—the street was simply closed to traffic except for deliveries at specified hours. No major reconstruction of the city was required. The most complete application of this idea (not counting Venice, which has had pedestrian precincts all along) is probably the pedestrian precinct in central Munich, Germany.

The idea of a pedestrian district for a central shopping area has now become something of an urban design commonplace. The prototype for many cities has not been the mall in Kalamazoo but the transitway on Nicollet Avenue in Minneapolis (completed in 1967), where a traffic lane in each direction is kept open for

Opposite: in Europe, extensive pedestrian precincts have been used to humanize the urban environment, particularly in old cities whose streets do not easily accept automobiles in any case. Until recently there has been little suburban competition with these city centers, and they are supported by much stronger public transportation networks than are usually found in the United States. This map shows the extent of the pedestrian network in Munich, Germany.

Top: The Marienplatz in central Munich. Note entrances to transit stations and bus stop glimpsed in foreground. Bottom: the diagram shows the rapid transit system supporting the pedestrian precinct of which the Marienplatz is a part.

ELEMENTS OF A DESIGN AND DEVELOPMENT STRATEGY

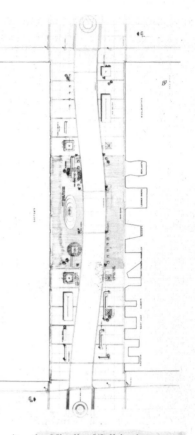

buses. The theory is that pedestrianization helps older downtowns to compete with the attractions of the newer suburban shopping centers. Unfortunately, an attractive public open space, by itself, is not sufficient to arrest the decline of a central shopping district. Parking, public transportation, and coordinated management for stores are all of great importance, as is imaginative retailing in general. However, there is no question that an attractively designed series of public spaces can have a positive effect on retailing; urban design does have a direct economic benefit.

Streets in residential districts can also be the basis of public open-space improvements. Many residential streets are much too wide, and—at the same time—do not provide a sufficient buffer between residences and traffic. Governmental standards frequently prescribed the same criteria whether the street's function was as a major arterial, a collector street, or simply to give access to a small number of houses. An existing street network can be replanned to differentiate the function of streets. Putting up barriers can make a street into a cul-de-sac, changing its function to being only a means of access to the properties along the street itself. After this change of function, unneeded width can be turned into landscaped park space, parking, or a combination

Opposite: the Nicollet Mall in downtown Minneapolis, the most successful downtown mall in the United States. Above left: detail of a bus shelter and above a plan of a typical block. The planners were Barton-Aschman Associates, the landscape architect Lawrence Halprin & Associates. The serpentine roadway—for buses only—permits relatively large pedestrian areas to be created on alternating sides of the street. The trees are probably the most important element in the design.

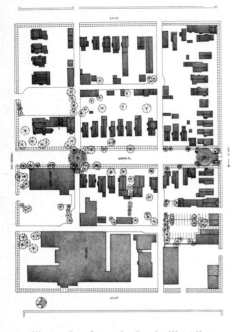

An illustration from the Louisville Alley Study shows the effect of closing one end of a street in a residential neighborhood, creating a situation analogous to a suburban cul-de-sac. Turning circles to be inlaid in the pavement are for the guidance of motorists. Planners were the Louisville Community Design Center, Jonathan Barnett, consultant.

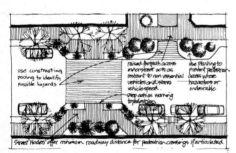

An illustration of street improvements in Adelaide, Australia, where excessively wide rights of way have been re-used to provide landscaping and recreation space. Planners are Llewelyn-Davies, Kinhill.

of both. Streets that are seen to function only as collector streets can also have their trafficways reduced and the extra space landscaped.

A comprehensive program of street improvements that created loop access streets and collector streets, which could not be used for through traffic out of a conventional street grid, was proposed as part of the San Francisco Urban Design Plan (see Chapter 8). The proposal was backed up by a study by Donald Appleyard and Mark Lintell which showed that a sense of community among neighbors along a street was created in an inverse ratio to the amount of traffic on the street. There has been severe community opposition to carrying out such improvements, however. The slogan, "Streets for people and not for automobiles," which is so often on the lips of well-intentioned planners, is an oversimplification. Automobiles are owned by people, who resist losing an accustomed parking space or having to change their route to work.

Nevertheless, redesigning streets can be an important means of improving residential neighborhoods, as is

PLAN FOR PROTECTED RESIDENTIAL AREAS

ELEMENTS OF A DESIGN AND DEVELOPMENT STRATEGY

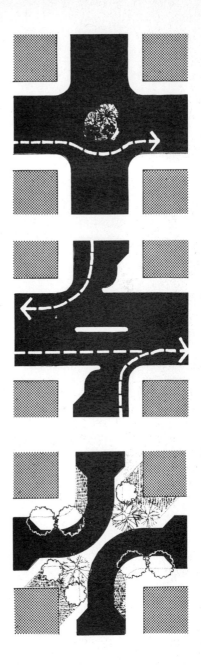

Opposite: map of San Francisco, from the San Francisco Urban Design Plan, showing the major streets. The establishment of such a street hierarchy permits less important streets to be narrowed or even closed.

Above: illustrations from the San Francisco Urban Design Plan showing different methods of closing or narrowing gridiron plan streets in residential neighborhoods.

Top: view of Freeway Park in downtown Seattle, Washington, designed by Lawrence Halprin & Associates, which bridges over an expressway right-of-way connecting parts of the city that had been separated by the highway construction.

Above: detail of Seattle's Freeway Park

shown in the examples on page 172 from Louisville, Kentucky, and Adelaide, Australia.

Another set of public open-space issues is created by the plaza and public open-space requirements that are written into many zoning ordinances. As we saw in Chapter 5, encouraging or requiring a plaza as part of each building project promotes a disconnected series of spaces that may not relate well to each other or to the basic character of the city. Another problem with these legislated plazas has been that the laws have not specified that the plazas be pleasant and usable. Many of them are neither.

If zoning regulations are to be used as a means of assigning the cost of creating public open space to private real estate investment, then language is needed in the regulations that will specify and coordinate locations. There are several different ways of accomplishing this objective, none of which is perfect. One method is through special district mapping, as in the Greenwich

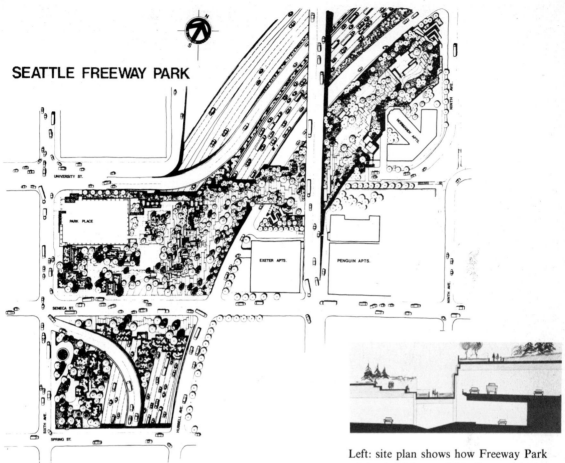

SEATTLE FREEWAY PARK

Left: site plan shows how Freeway Park relates to highway right-of-way and ramps. Above: cross-sections explain the relation of part to highway. Below: an aerial photograph taken before the part was constructed shows how the freeway slices through the fabric of the city.

Street or Manhattan Landing special districts described in Chapter 6. A second method is through mandatory standards and/or a point system of zoning incentives; a third is by establishing standards for discretionary design review. Both of these methods are described in Chapter 14.

An alternate method of controlling the location of public open space is for government to take on the capital costs for a public open space, and get these costs back from the private sector in the form of increased property taxes. The rationale behind this concept is that the public space creates an increase in real estate values for the properties that adjoin it. This value can be taxed, and the resultant income stream used to pay back the

A map of the development district related to the Loring Park Extension. This park was financed by the tax-increment method described in Chapter 15. A related housing development is shown in Chapters 10 and 15.

ELEMENTS OF A DESIGN AND DEVELOPMENT STRATEGY

GREENWAY SITE PLAN
LORING PARK

The Loring Park Extension in downtown Minneapolis connects the Nicolet Mall to the existing Loring Park. This public open-space investment not only gives new coherence to the city but creates valuable frontages for adjacent property. The planners and landscape architects were M. Paul Friedberg & Associates.

Peavey Plaza, next to Orchestra Hall, at the end of the Nicollet Mall where it meets the Loring Park Extension. The site of both this park and the concert hall represent additional segments of a coherent public open-space and investment strategy. The landscape architects were M. Paul Friedberg & Associates.

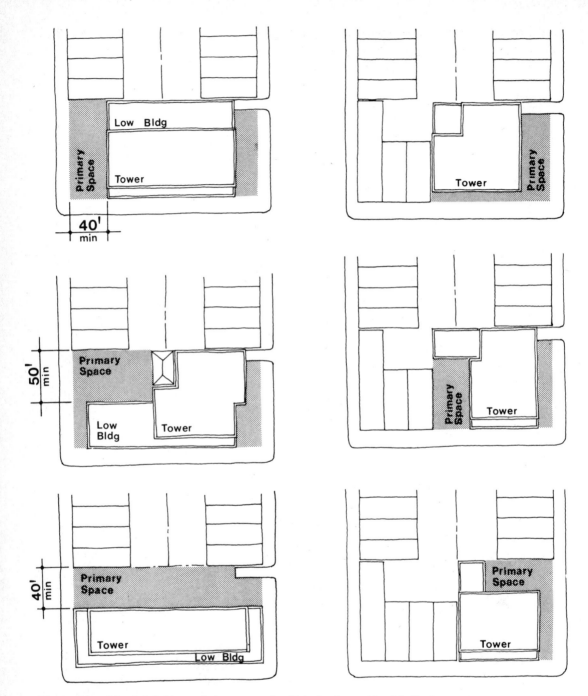

Illustrations of legal definitions of plaza space for high-density residential districts in New York City. The intention of these regulations is to ensure that such public open space provided by developers in response to zoning incentives will actually be usable by the public.

ELEMENTS OF A DESIGN AND DEVELOPMENT STRATEGY

capital costs of the public open space. The technique is known as tax-increment financing, and we will come back to it in Chapter 15. Its significance here is that direct investment permits the public to control the location and design of the public space.

A public investment in open space may also return more general economic benefits, which go beyond advantages for the immediately adjacent properties. The Freeway Park in Seattle is an example of this kind of public open-space investment. It helps correct a serious urban design mistake—when a freeway was cut right through the central business district of the city. The park that bridges over the freeway makes a start at knitting the city together again. Analogous investments in river and harbor frontages, replacing disused docks and railway tracks, perform the same corrective function.

The usability of public open space is a related, but somewhat different question. The city of Minneapolis could control the design of the Loring Park Extension, which was created through tax-increment financing. But what about the spaces that are created as a result of zoning requirements? These spaces are often inhospitable, not because their designers were stupid but because the owners of the building, out of a concern for insurance and maintenance costs, deliberately sought an environment that encouraged people to admire the building briefly and then be on their way.

An important prototype for legislation that encourages more usable plazas was enacted by New York City in 1975 and in 1976. The legislation, which applies to high-density residential and commercial districts in Manhattan, was prepared by the Urban Design Group of the City Planning Department, working with William H. Whyte. Whyte—and more recently the Project for Public Spaces, which he helped to found—has analyzed the way people use plaza spaces, by means of interviews, films, and time-lapse photography, among other techniques.

The New York legislation for residential districts distinguishes between plazas that are located along commercial frontages and plazas in purely residential

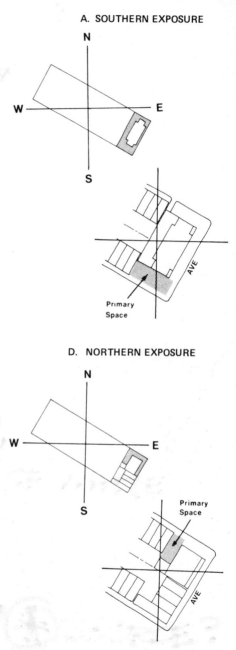

Other illustrations of legal requirements for plazas that receive zoning bonuses in New York City; these regulations deal with the orientation of primary spaces.

Opposite: the Crystal Court of the IDS Building in Minneapolis, which serves as the hub of the city's pedestrian bridge system. Architects of the building were Philip Johnson & John Burgee.

Below: the official Minneapolis plan, which relates the pedestrian bridge system ("Skyways") to the rest of the proposed transportation network.

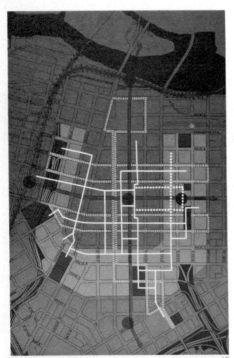

Circulation and Transit Plan
- Skyways
- Underground Concourses
- Minibus Route
- Mechanical Distributor and/or Transit Tunnel
- Rapid Transit Route
- Fringe Parking Area
- Fringe Parking Ramps
- Rapid Transit Stations

areas. On commercial streets, continuity along retail frontages is a primary requirement. "Continuity" is defined in two ways: by both use and placement. Store frontages are required to have retail tenants in half the commercial frontage, restricting the space available to offices, clubs, and banks. The placement of commercial frontage is also encouraged to continue existing shopping patterns, by being at the building line, for example.

The plaza itself is categorized according to three different kinds of space: primary space, residual space, and a northern plaza. The primary space must be at least 60 percent of the building's total plaza area, and the space is defined in such a way that a sidewalk widening around the whole street perimeter of the building will not satisfy the requirements. Orientation of the plaza is specified in the regulations so that, in as many cases as possible, the plaza will receive a significant amount of sunlight. In the case of building lots where such orientation is not possible, northern plazas, there are compensating requirements. There are also provisions that encourage the usability of plazas in a more particular way, such as minimum requirements for built-in seating, and definitions of acceptable amenities like bicycle racks and drinking fountains.

Recognizing some of the reasons why plaza designs have not been hospitable to public use in the past, the regulations do permit primary plaza spaces to be closed off at night. However, the overall sense of the regulations is to hold the building owner to clearly expressed, detailed standards of design and operation. The legislation was passed without significant opposition at the bottom of New York City's mid-1970s real estate depression, when developers had more pressing problems on their minds than the investment climate for future buildings. If the rules stay on the books, they will make a big difference to future plaza design.

Public open spaces can be indoors as well as outdoors, and can take the form of networks of underground connections or of pedestrian bridges. The underground concourse system in Montreal is a famous example, as are the underground concourses to be found in Tokyo and Osaka. The skyway system in Min-

Right: interior of Citicorp's public space. Below: the external plaza of the Citicorp Building, showing how level changes lead to an entrance to the subway system. The building at left is St. Peter's Church. Architects for both the building and the church were Hugh Stubbins & Associates.

ELEMENTS OF A DESIGN AND DEVELOPMENT STRATEGY

neapolis or the similar system in St. Paul are good examples of the way pedestrian bridges can be used in a city. The separation of pedestrian and automobile traffic onto different levels used to be axiomatic among planners and architects, something self-evidently desirable. There is a major problem with this concept, however, that has emerged when examples have actually been carried out. Pedestrian circulation is the life blood of the retailing system. If nobody walks by a storefront, the store is not going to be worth much. Except in the densest of retail areas, multi-level pedestrian circulation runs the risk of dividing the flow of people in such a way as to diminish the value of all retail frontage. Alternatively, one level may become dominant at the expense of the others.

A skyway or concourse system should thus not be introduced into a retail district unless everyone concerned is clear about just what its purpose is and what the effect will be if the plan succeeds.

Large internal spaces introduced into the city as retail concourses also create the risk of diminishing the value of traditional street frontages. The old-fashioned arcade leads shoppers from one street to another. The new downtown shopping mall, on the model established by Victor Gruen for the Midtown Plaza in Rochester, New York, may internalize shopping completely. People enter the mall directly from a garage and do not have to go out on the streets at all. The ZCMI and Crossroads centers, recently completed in Salt Lake City, have clearly had a negative effect on traditional shopping locations. On the other hand, the net gain in comparison-goods retailing for the city center has been a strong one, making the trade-off worthwhile from the city's point of view.

In areas of the city center that are not prime retail locations, an internal public space may be worth more to the public than a plaza. The public space in the Citicorp Center was built under a zoning regulation that permitted comparable floor-area increases for an indoor pedestrian space as for an outdoor plaza. The covered pedestrian space at 100 William Street is another New York example, as is the space for a branch

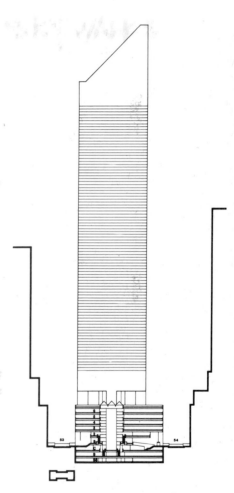

A section through the Citicorp Building in New York City, showing the covered pedestrian space that gave the building a floor-area bonus under the zoning regulations.

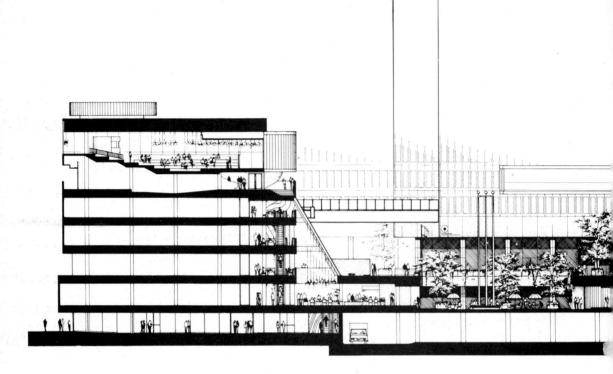

Section perspective through Peachtree Center in Atlanta, Georgia, showing how public open spaces are integrated with different components of the complex and with the city's transit system. Architects were John Portman & Associates.

of the Bronx Botanic Garden that is part of the IBM Building, and the Whitney Museum sculpture gallery, which is part of the Philip Morris headquarters. As discussed in Chapter 7, these last two public spaces were part of a progressive relaxation of zoning requirements that permitted bulkier and bulkier buildings on smaller and smaller sites. The public spaces themselves, however, are unquestionably more beneficial than traditional plazas would have been. As long as the trade-offs are understood, an internal public space makes good sense as one of the components of a public open-space policy.

In the long run, the effectiveness of public open space is related to how well such spaces are integrated into the overall design of the city. Peachtree Center in Atlanta provides a good example of the integration of various kinds of public open space, none especially impressive

ELEMENTS OF A DESIGN AND DEVELOPMENT STRATEGY

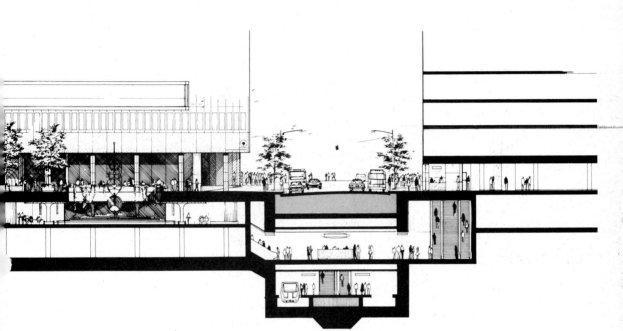

by itself, into a smoothly working system that combines hotels, shopping, a theater, and office space. There are underground concourse connections to the rapid transit system, pedestrian bridges, grade-level plazas, sunken plazas, and a greenhouse-like covered space, all working together as shown in the section perspective above.

At Peachtree Center, this integration was achieved because all the property was controlled by the architect-developer, John Portman. In other locations, similar connections are possible, if we can work out the mechanisms for cooperation between local government and the private investor. The development along Market Street in San Francisco may be the largest-scale example of the integration of public and private open space to date. A series of spaces is created, relating both to the street and to the entrances to the BART system. All that is required is the public determination to achieve

Plaza in San Francisco leading to Bay Area Rapid Transit System (BART) under Market Street. The relationship of a remodeled Market Street to various public open spaces is one of the largest-scale urban design improvements in any American city.

this type of integration: almost all the expenditure would have taken place in any case, whether as part of the rapid transit system, as part of the individual buildings, or as part of the municipally funded street improvements.

ELEMENTS OF A DESIGN AND DEVELOPMENT STRATEGY

12

Standards for Street Furniture, Lighting, and Signs

In most cities something like a quarter of the land area is used for streets, the percentage varying with the nature of the street layout. In an older central business district with a grid of relatively short blocks the percentage will be higher; in a low-density residential area with narrow, winding roads the percentage will be lower. By any measurement, however, streets make up a significant portion of our surroundings.

If a city is to be designed, the design of the streets, and the streetscape, are both going to have a significant effect.

In most cities it is too late to change the basic street layout. In a few cases streets may have been planned as part of an overall design, as in Savannah, Georgia; Washington, D.C.; parts of Paris; or Canberra, the planned capital of Australia. Usually, however, streets have been laid out by a surveyor in an earlier and simpler time, before modern traffic and intensive land development were ever imagined. What the surveyor was trying to do was create an efficient method of giving access to the maximum number of lots, which were expected to be developed into houses or even farms. In other cities the street pattern may be a relic of an earlier pattern of country lanes.

If you look at an old engraving of a city, the streets generally appear as empty spaces between buildings. There are a few people in carriages, perhaps, or even

Street lights, traffic signals, and other street furniture have a strong influence on the design of cities.

crowds and traffic, but few permanent objects. In a nineteenth-century view there may well be street trees arching over the trafficway. Most of these views are idealized. The artist left out the horse manure and the flies; but the sense you have of looking at a lost world comes at least partly from the uncluttered appearance of the street. No overhead electric and telephone wires and poles, few street lights, no parking meters, street signs, traffic signals, highway information signs, fire hydrants, fire and police call boxes, mail collection boxes, telephone booths, newspaper vending machines, trash baskets, and so on. If there were once any trees, they have probably been cut down to make way for more traffic lanes, or because trees obstructed the motorist's view of traffic entering from side streets. The trees to be seen in today's streets are little, stunted growths. Poisoned by exhaust gases, assaulted by delivery trucks, cut away from wires and signs, trees on downtown streets seldom survive to maturity these days, except along specially designed malls—of which more later.

The various objects that clutter up our streets have almost always been added over time without any particular plan, much as if one had furnished a room with a random collection of beds, chairs, and kitchen appliances. Street lights, traffic signals, trash baskets, and the like are in fact generally referred to as street furniture. The lack of any organizing concept or decorative plan for street furniture produces visual chaos.

Because we are so used to street signs and traffic signals, we don't pay any attention to their incoherent design and chaotic arrangement, just as people who live near a noisy factory learn to ignore the sounds of industrial processes. However, in the back of their minds, the neighbors know the factory is operating. When the noise stops, or the appurtenances of the street are well arranged, we become aware of the difference.

Street lights and traffic signals, particularly in central business districts, represent big expenditures by local government. Frequently whole districts are given new and brighter street lamps—or a computerized system of traffic signals. New lights are installed, new traffic sig-

ELEMENTS OF A DESIGN AND DEVELOPMENT STRATEGY

nals put up. Millions of dollars are spent on this hardware, and because no one is thinking about the design of the street, the opportunity is lost to make any improvement in the overall appearance of the city. Frequently the street looks even worse, because new elements have been added to the existing jumble.

As stated earlier, the routine reconstruction of streets for maintenance reasons is another big local expenditure. The pavement is taken up, curbs frequently are replaced, utility access points leveled, new pavement put down, and the street ends up looking exactly as it did before. These big expenditures on new street furniture and paving could easily have had an enormous effect on the design of the city. It would cost very little more and the public would benefit greatly.

In order to improve the design of the street, however, we must first understand the reasons why things are done the way they are. As is so often the case in cities, it is only the overall result that is random and unconsidered; the individual decisions that lead to the chaos are all perfectly reasonable. If you want to make changes, it is necessary to deal with the functions and economics of street design.

Many advocates of good design seem to wish to get rid of modern street lighting and traffic control devices entirely. They have a tendency to equate good street furniture with the lamps and signs of the Edwardian period. Old-fashioned street lights, shaped like ornate cast-iron flowers, do have a definite charm, but their appeal in old photographs also has much to do with their sparse placement and the lack of other kinds of clutter.

In the "good old days," it was cheaper to have a policeman at every corner than to put up traffic signals, even after the technology for electric street lights was invented. In the good old days, there were usually fewer vehicles, road speeds were slower, and people were more likely to know their route, so that they did not need to rely on signs to find their way.

Thus there are few useful historic precedents for traffic signals, traffic information signs, or notices about parking; and street lights designed for gas do not per-

The Key to an Orderly Street Environment

form well when used to produce the levels of illumination that traffic engineers consider necessary for modern streets.

We have to devise our own solutions. Fortunately, much research into street lighting and street furniture improvements has already taken place. Cities wishing to improve their street design do not need to invent or employ untested systems.

The key to creating an orderly street environment is to use a new, rationalized lighting system as the armature for traffic signals and signs.

In central areas the lighting system must perform two functions: providing safe illumination for streets and a pleasant ambiance for the sidewalks. The common practice in lighting city centers has been to use a single fixture to do both jobs. Technological improvements have gone toward reducing the costs of installation, resulting in brighter and brighter lights on higher and higher poles, farther and farther apart. By concentrating on this definition of economy, many cities have produced a system in which there is always a glare in the eyes of motorists and a ghastly glow on the sidewalk that causes people to look and feel uncomfortable.

Two different kinds of lighting fixture are required. For the street itself, we need a fixture that gives a directed beam of light with the source "cut off," that is, hidden from view unless you are looking directly up at the light fixture. In this way the glare problem for motorists is almost eliminated. For the sidewalk, a lower, more decorative light fixture is needed, closer in spirit to those Edwardian street lamps. For pedestrian lighting, there is some psychological importance to having a visible light source. Where cut-off fixtures have been used for sidewalk lighting, there are complaints about the street being dark—even when an engineer with a light meter can prove that it isn't. A series of relatively low fixtures with an opaque white globe provides the reassurance of a visible light source and a good ambiance for pedestrians, the only difficulty being that a new source of glare is introduced. A globe light with an internal diffuser that directs light to the sidewalk and to the lower floors of surrounding buildings is a better

"Before" and "after" map of two blocks in downtown Pittsburgh, showing how a new system reduces the amount of clutter on the block by consolidation and systematization. The system was developed by the Pittsburgh Department of Planning, Fred P. Swiss, urban designer, Jonathan Barnett, consultant.

ELEMENTS OF A DESIGN AND DEVELOPMENT STRATEGY

answer, because the light source is hidden and no glare is created.

There should also be a distinction between the lighting at street intersections and that along the mid-blocks, as such a contrast is a safety factor for both drivers and pedestrians.

A sensible lighting system for a downtown area would thus have tall poles with cut-off fixtures at the intersections. On a wide street, tall poles with cut-off fixtures lighting the cartway would alternate with lower ornamental fixtures lighting the sidewalk. On narrower streets, the lower fixtures can light both the sidewalk and the cartway between intersections, provided that the ornamental fixture is equipped with a diffuser to eliminate glare and direct the light to the right place. While the capital costs for such a system are higher than the conventional arrangement, the operating costs may often be lower, as shorter fixtures, spaced more frequently, need less powerful light sources. Two 150-watt fixtures can do the work of one conventional 400-watt street light.

The rationalized lighting described above creates the opportunity to rationalize the street sign system and traffic information system as well. A typical method of placing traffic lights is on special poles, situated at corners. Alternatively, traffic lights may be bracketed to a light pole, if one is handy. On wide streets, federal standards now require traffic lights out over the lanes of traffic. One rough-and-ready method is to sling the lights across the intersection on wires. A more permanent installation would have the signals dangling from a boom that is cantilevered across the intersection. We are habituated to seeing them, but these traffic signal booms are some of the most unappealing objects to be found in a city. The boom is usually set at an angle, then guyed back to the pole by two wires. The signal is free to swing back and forth in the wind, and may be hard to see amid the profusion of other signs and lights that make up the streetscape. As a result, traffic engineers suggest larger and larger signal lights for intersections on important streets, which makes the whole apparatus less appealing than ever.

Intersection Wood·Fifth·Oliver Existing

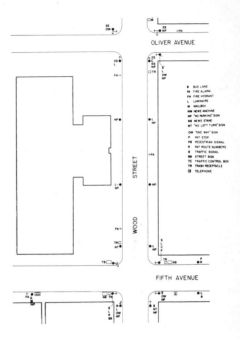

Intersection Wood·Fifth·Oliver Proposed

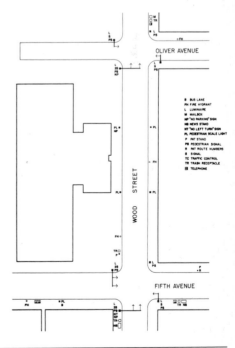

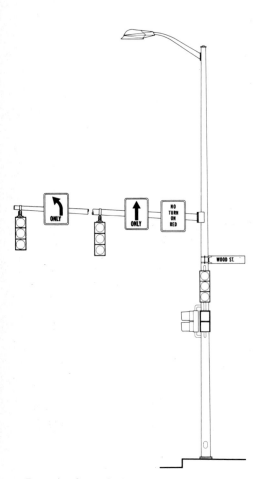

A better answer is to use the tall light poles that should occur at intersections in any case as the support structure for a frame—not a boom—which is cantilevered across the intersection on a straight line, not a diagonal. This frame houses the traffic signals and creates an orderly neutral background for them, enhancing their visibility. It also provides a place for all the signs, "No turn on red," "Left lane must turn left," and so on, which are usually bracketed to light poles or left swinging crazily from the traffic light booms. With a little forethought, street signs, one-way signs, and route signs can also be incorporated into the frame. On the mid-blocks, parking information signs and bus route signs, which frequently have little poles of their own, can be attached to the lamp standards, which occur more often than the widely spaced tall poles that have become conventional in recent years. The lamp standards should be tapped to permit signs to be placed only at predetermined locations. Sign sizes should be standardized. Where additional parking signs are needed between lamp standards, a simple frame can be introduced for them.

It is important that the organization and placement of signs follow such a system if the full effect of an improved streetscape is to be felt. What happens in most cities when a new sign is needed is that the sign shop makes it up, and a work crew goes out and either brackets it to a light pole or puts up a separate structure for it. All the placement decisions are made on an ad hoc basis, rarely with any sense of the design of the street. Again, once a rationalized lighting and sign system has been introduced, it is important to create the administrative procedures to go with it, otherwise, over time, additional signs will be introduced ad hoc, and the overall quality of the system will be diminished.

The following illustrations show the rationalized lighting and sign system worked out for downtown Pittsburgh. It is presented the way it was to authorities there: first the nondescript collection of poles, lights, and signs that were to be seen on downtown streets; then the replacements that might be ordered routinely; and finally a designed system. The cost figures show that

Portrait of a typical center city light post with a boom for traffic signals and signs. The light fixture throws glare into eyes of oncoming motorists and casts a similar glare on intersections and on the mid-block cartway and the sidewalks. Signs and traffic signals are attached with bands, which is an invitation to ad-hoc design decisions by personnel doing the installation. Regulations requiring a signal related to each traffic lane have made this light, sign and signal complex into a prominent element of the city, without many people being aware of what was happening.

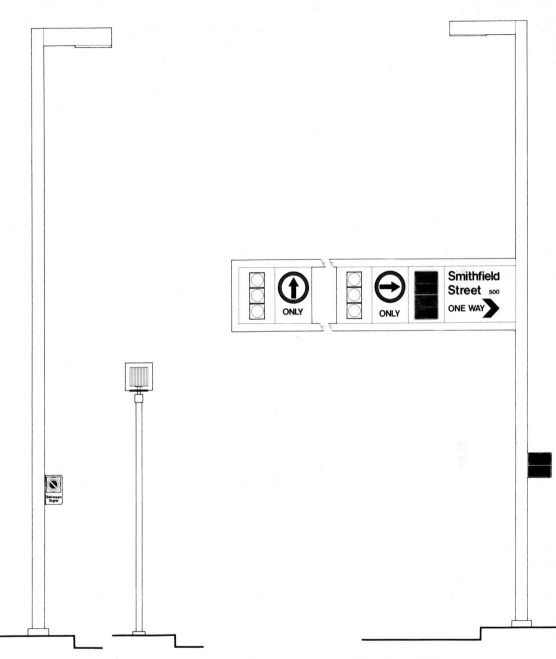

Smithfield
Street 500
ONE WAY ▶

A coordinated street lighting, traffic signal, and graphic information system designed for downtown Pittsburgh from components already being manufactured. The street light design has a cut-off fixture that reduces glare; the frame organizes traffic signals and signs so that they are coherent and easily distinguished from other signs and lights; a separate fixture for mid-block sidewalks and streets has a clear globe with a cut-off fixture to eliminate glare and gives a different light from high fixture. Poles are tapped with predrilled holes for signals and signs, and policies discourage the attachment of fixtures with bands.

View along Liberty Road in suburban
Baltimore, showing a typical American
roadscape, with overhead utility wires,
conflicting signs, and traffic signals slung
across the intersection on wires. Opposite:
The proposals for Liberty Road developed
by Ben-Ami Friedman Associates, urban
designers, would bury wires, organize signs
and signals.

there is a premium to be paid for a designed system, but
the increment involved is not large compared to the
improvement obtained. To replace all the existing light
poles, light signals, and signs downtown would cost
about $1,650,000 in 1980 dollars for the conventional
"hardware" shown in the drawings; the improved system, by contrast, would cost about $3,325,000, again in
1980 dollars. Yes, the new system does cost twice as
much; but the hardware component of the street reconstruction is a very small component of the total cost. A
little over $1.5 million does not seem a big premium to
pay in a large city downtown to achieve a complete
rationalization of the lighting and sign system. It is
within the reach of private philanthropy or contributions by downtown business interests.

The following illustrations are for an analogous system designed for a suburban commercial strip on Liberty Road, northeast of Baltimore. The principle is similar, but the scale is necessarily larger. Telephone and
electric wires are placed in underground conduits in
most downtowns, but not on suburban strip shopping
streets. The system shown here requires all the wires to
be buried, which is a very expensive process. An alternative approach would be to rationalize the wiring, by
designing the way it is placed on the poles, and using
the poles for other purposes, such as advertising signs
for roadside businesses. Such measures would reduce
the number of sign poles, and place advertising signs on
the same kind of orderly modular system suggested for
traffic signs.

In suburban residential areas where streets are lined
with trees and there are few traffic lights or signs, the
usual ad hoc method of placing street lamps on telephone poles may continue to be perfectly acceptable.
However, in new subdivisions, it makes sense to require
street lights with cut-off light sources, and to specify
cut-off fixtures when replacement street lights are installed in existing areas. Of course, wherever electrical
service and telephone wires can be buried, big improvements in the streetscape are created.

Fire and police alarms and even postal collection
boxes can be incorporated into a rationalized lighting

(Pages 195, 196) Street furniture and details
of sign and signal system for Liberty Road.
The most important, and most difficult,
proposal is to bury the utility wires.

ELEMENTS OF A DESIGN AND DEVELOPMENT STRATEGY

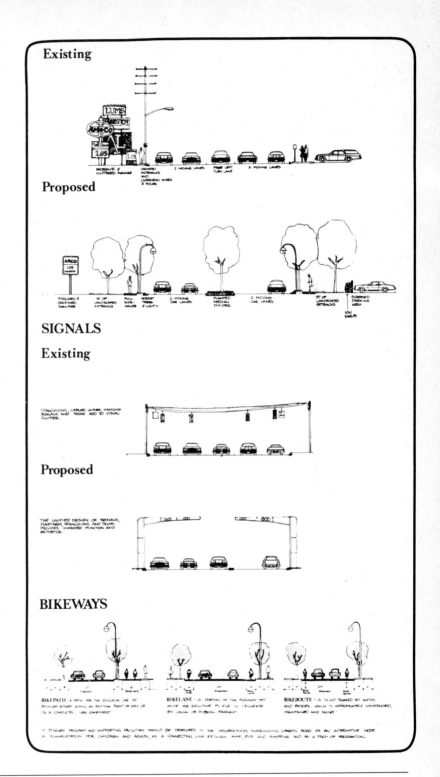

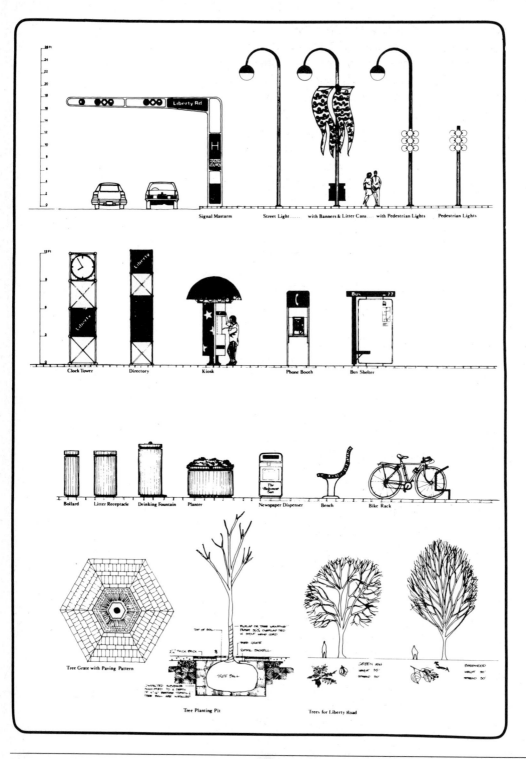

Signal Mastarm Street Light...... with Banners & Litter Cans.... with Pedestrian Lights Pedestrian Lights

Clock Tower Directory Kiosk Phone Booth Bus Shelter

Bollard Litter Receptacle Drinking Fountain Planter Newspaper Dispenser Bench Bike Rack

Tree Grate with Paving Pattern

Tree Planting Pit

Trees for Liberty Road

ELEMENTS OF A DESIGN AND DEVELOPMENT STRATEGY

and sign system if the administrative problems can be solved. But there are some elements of street furniture that must be considered separately, including bus shelters, and wastebaskets. The bus shelters developed for New York City by a private company are a good example of what a well-designed shelter can look like. In this instance, the capital cost and maintenance of the shelters—and presumably a profit for the entrepreneurs—all come from advertising revenues. Alternatively, a smaller display area could be devoted to bus route information instead of commercial messages, and the costs borne by the public. Well-designed armatures for wastepaper baskets and newspaper vending machines have also been developed, as shown in the illustrations at left.

In most places the capital cost of the sidewalk is the responsibility of the property owner, who must meet standards of construction established by local government. These standards can be amended to forbid asphalt sidewalks, for example, or to require granite curbs. A vocabulary of acceptable finishes and materials can be established to ensure congruity over time. Choice of finishes for streets and sidewalks should include a consideration of maintenance. What does the finish look like when discarded chewing gum sticks to the sidewalk; is the sidewalk slippery in winter; will the street show the oil drippings from cars?

Sidewalks can be designed with a strip of removable panels, or modular materials like bricks, running parallel to the curb. Pipes and wires can be placed below this strip, reducing the need to dig up whole sidewalks to make repairs. Trees and planting boxes can be designed as part of this strip, as shown in the illustration at left.

The important point to remember in connection with all of these streetscape improvements is that most of the capital cost is money that is going to be spent anyway. The increase in cost, where there is any, is always minute in comparison with the benefits gained. When a new traffic signal system is installed, when street lights are replaced, when new road signs are put up, when streets and sidewalks are rebuilt or repaired, these expendi-

Most of the capital cost is money that will be spent anyway.

Traffic signal and sign system on Market Street in downtown San Francisco. Walk/Don't Walk signals have street names on reverse sides. Circular traffic signal cases also have street names on the reverse side. The wooden poles, which support the wires for the trolley buses, will be removed.

tures should take place according to a designed system. If such a system is built into a locality's administrative and budgetary procedures, the whole public environment can be transformed over time.

ELEMENTS OF A DESIGN AND DEVELOPMENT STRATEGY

13

Transportation and
Urban Design Policy

Despite our new awareness that we could run out of
important natural resources, cities are likely to depend
on the car, the bus, and the truck as transportation for
a long time to come. Self-propelled wheeled transit systems have become so fundamental a part of the design
of our cities that the cost of changing to other means
of transport would be staggering. Inflation has brought
the capital cost of a new underground rail transit system to something like $100 million a mile; a surface rail
system could cost $20 million a mile. If such systems
are constructed in parts of cities that have developed in
the last fifty years, people will find that the locations of
houses, apartments, stores, and factories are not such
that a rail rapid transit system can serve them efficiently.

The same problem will be found if existing rail corridors are used for rapid transit. No one wanted to live
next to a railroad, so the railroad tends to be some
distance from the most important destinations. In cities
like Cleveland, which grew up in the railroad and
streetcar age, it is possible to improve existing rail rapid
transit and railroad installations; in the larger cities of
the railroad age, like New York, Chicago, and Boston,
rail rapid transit continues to be an important part of
the transportation system. In the San Francisco Bay
Area, or metropolitan Atlanta, or Washington, D.C.,
and Baltimore, a major investment in rail rapid transit

What About Innovative New Systems?

will make good sense over time. For the average American city, however, it is going to be the car, the bus, and the truck.

What about innovative new systems—people-movers, or PRT (personal rapid transit), or shuttle buses?

Well, maybe. A people-mover is essentially a moving sidewalk. The problem is, how do you get onto it without losing your footing? The answer seems to be that you can't run the moving belt at more than about three miles an hour. If you want to increase the speed, you have to add a second moving belt, running at, say, six miles an hour. You can then move from one to the other without losing your balance, because the difference in

Illustrations of a personal rapid transit system (PRT) from the study for the Denver Rapid Transit District by Wallace, McHarg, Roberts & Todd. PRTs still inspire some unanswered questions: Isn't the system reinventing the "El"; can passenger safety on driverless cars be guaranteed; does the automated technology work?

speed between the two belts is only three miles an hour. Fine, but how do you get off? Only at places where there is a second moving belt at the slower speed. Where does the belt system run? How does it cross streets? Do you really gain anything over the speed of ordinary walking?

The answer to these questions seems to be some special right of way, which in downtown areas (the only place except airports where there are the crowds necessary to justify the capital cost of a people-mover) would mean channeling pedestrians away from shop fronts onto a system where they cannot get on and off except at predetermined points. As pedestrian movement is the life blood of the retail system, skepticism about people-movers would seem to be in order. If you have used a people-mover at an airport, you will have noticed that the people who walk along beside you can move faster; your advantage is that you are able to put your suitcase down and still keep moving.

A people-mover is a horizontal escalator; a PRT car is often described as a horizontal elevator. The theory is that you would go to a PRT station, press a call button, and the next car that was going your way would stop for you. These cars would hold between ten and twenty people and would be automated, requiring no driver and thus saving much of the usual cost of operating rapid transit.

The voters of the Denver Rapid Transit District actually passed a bond issue to build such a system. The concept was presented as a decisive way to reduce the air pollution in the Denver metropolitan area. There are PRT systems in operation at a few big airports like those in Tampa, Dallas–Fort Worth, and Seattle; but no one has ever designed a system to deal with the complex routes to multiple destinations required in a city. It is not at all clear that the technology for the Denver PRT system actually existed. There were other problems. The PRT cars have to run on a guideway, and that guideway—in order to minimize conflicts with the street system—had to be elevated. It is not possible to suspend an active PRT system on a few gossamer strands: it needs substantial guide rails held up by powerful stanchions. While somewhat more pleasing in appearance than the elevated railways that used to disfigure city streets, the PRT system is still very much the same thing as an "El." Most people were just congratulating themselves for at last getting rid of Els, and here they were sneaking back into the city again. The residents of Denver's more expensive residential areas made it clear that they wanted no PRT guideways near them. If the PRT couldn't run where most car users wanted to go, there wasn't much point in it.

There was another question: would a young woman, or an elderly person, or anyone else who felt vulnerable and was traveling alone, venture onto an unattended, automated PRT car, particularly at night? An elevator can be dangerous enough; but this kind of horizontal elevator, with its long runs between stations, could be the setting for a horror story. Yes, there could be closed-circuit television to some central point, but that was relatively small comfort, particularly when a hand or a piece of tape can be put over a lens. Denver, like most places which are big enough to support a PRT system, has a high crime rate. Could a PRT system ever be made safe?

Well then, what about the shuttle bus? It is easy enough to draw them on a map. Here is the peripheral parking lot, and here, along this dotted line, is the shuttle bus to downtown. Question: How often does the shuttle run? If the shuttle is to run every five minutes, and the route for the shuttle takes half an hour, that means six buses are needed. As transit rush hours take place at the beginning and end of a working day, that means two shifts of drivers. Then there are relief drivers, so that the regular drivers can take breaks during the day; spare buses, and a staff to repair them. You get the idea. Running a shuttle-bus system is expensive, if it is to run frequently enough to attract a substantial ridership.

If a shuttle runs only between two or three fixed points, and it is possible to build a guideway, this may be a feasible situation for a PRT. The cable car between Roosevelt Island and Manhattan is a successful example. But there aren't very many of them.

An aerial photograph of the model, designed by Norman Bel Geddes, created for the General Motors Pavilion at the New York World's Fair of 1939. Called the *World of 1960*, it is a prediction of land development created by the automobile that has proved astonishingly accurate. Except for the separation of tall buildings, this could be a photograph of almost any large American city today.

ELEMENTS OF A DESIGN AND DEVELOPMENT STRATEGY

So, it is back to the car, the ordinary bus route, and the truck. The effect of such self-propelled vehicles on city design was foreseen by Le Corbusier in his Voisin Plan, by Frank Lloyd Wright in his Broadacre City formulation, and by Norman Bel Geddes in the model of the city of 1960 that he designed for the Futurama Exhibit in the General Motors Pavilion at the World's Fair of 1939. It was Bel Geddes's vision that turned out to be the most prophetic, probably because the main design determinations were measures to make automobile traffic flow more smoothly. At the heart of his city were the confluences of huge multi-level expressways; other, lesser expressways crisscrossed the city at a lower level, while ordinary streets were carried across on bridges. Each city block was a disassociated element, surrounded by high-speed access systems. Streamlined towers rose from some of these blocks, while others continued to house fragments of the past: a church, smaller buildings, a park. The Bunker Hill renewal district in downtown Los Angeles has ended up looking very nearly like the Futurama model, and large fragments of Bel Geddes's vision can be seen in most American cities. What has prevented Bel Geddes from being even more prophetic is the resistance of existing businesses, particularly retailing, and the property values of existing buildings.

Today we are grateful for the inertia in our commercial and real estate systems, for we have come to realize that a city designed solely for the movement of self-propelled vehicles is a city where historic preservation is very difficult and traditional street life almost impossible.

It is true that the streets in most of our city centers were laid out for the horse and buggy, without any pre-vision of the skyscraper and consequent higher densities of people and vehicles that we find in the heart of our cities today. On the other hand, we have learned that traffic follows something very much like Parkinson's Law. Professor Parkinson stated, as you remember, the following profound truth about human nature: "Work expands to fill the time allotted to it." His book was humorously written, but the observation is a seri-

ELEMENTS OF A DESIGN AND DEVELOPMENT STRATEGY

ous one. Traffic also expands, to congest the roadways allotted to it. The city of Los Angeles has been equipped with a magnificent collection of freeways; but the better the freeway system worked, the more people were attracted to using it. Slicing through our city centers to accommodate the automobile not only destroys traditional urban values; it may not even work.

What we come to instead is a form of compromise. We need expressways to give access to city centers, and to permit traffic not bound for the city center to go by it. But, once these basic objectives are attained, we should not strive for complete perfection of vehicular movement, lest we destroy the city that was the destination in the first place.

The name often given to this compromise is "traffic systems management." Automobile traffic, parking, bus routes, and truck traffic should all be considered to be parts of a series of related decisions. Before making improvements in one element, the effect on the other parts of the traffic picture should be considered. In addition, the existing city is accepted as the context for traffic systems management; the measures proposed must be tested for their effect on retailing, or historic preservation, or the general ambiance and quality of city life.

Traffic systems management is, however, a definition of a method of solving problems rather than a formula for a set of tried-and-true results. It is the traffic engineers' way of saying that the movement systems of a city are a matter of urban design.

For example, the number of parking places provided on a given block should be related to the number of parking places in the downtown area as a whole, as should the mix of parking provided: that is, whether the rates encourage short-term or long-term parking. If the parking is considered as a system, and the current rates of traffic flow on streets are understood, it is possible to say with some objectivity that a parking garage of a given number of spaces is, or is not, appropriate at a particular location.

Another example: the reasons why traffic backs up at a particular intersection can be analyzed. It may not be

Traffic Systems Management

necessary to add another lane. The problem might be traced to the timing of the traffic light cycle; or the radius of curvature at the corner might be causing buses to swing out into a second lane in order to make a turn. Traffic systems management involves a series of such adjustments as changing light cycles and modifying corners, which add up to greater capacity for the street system without removing sidewalks and buildings.

Each component of the traffic mix should also be understood as a system. Bus routes are often the result of historical factors dating back to the time when several competing transit companies served the city center. These days the buses are almost certainly under a single government ownership, and there is an opportunity to rationalize routes and frequency of service. It is also possible to create systems of express buses, which have some of the speed associated with rail rapid transit but much more flexibility in designing the location of stops where passengers get on and off. In Pittsburgh, two new busways have been created. The buses pick up passengers in the usual way, then proceed downtown nonstop, running for part of the distance on an exclusive right of way. Once the buses enter downtown, they follow a loop through the street system, letting passengers off near their destinations just like the other buses. The right of way for the East Bus Way has been created in part by paving over disused railway tracks. In other cities, busways have been created during rush hours by taking a lane out of an expressway, usually on the side away from peak hour traffic, creating what is known as a contra-flow bus lane.

Truck traffic also constitutes a system, or a series of systems. As inter-city trailer trucks have gotten bigger and bigger, their presence in city center streets has become more and more disruptive. It is a problem that has grown up gradually, so that many people still do not perceive it. Trucks that are simply taking shortcuts through downtown streets in order to reach other destinations should be discouraged from doing so. If the problems with trade unions can be worked out, restricting deliveries to non-rush hours can also improve the way the traffic system works.

ELEMENTS OF A DESIGN AND DEVELOPMENT STRATEGY

The design and placement of truck docks is another important issue. Locating the truck docks on the correct streets, and making them large enough to take in the whole truck, can have an important effect on traffic. Ideally, truck docks should be centralized, and connected to the buildings they service by tunnels. The Livingston-Bond Parking Garage in downtown Brooklyn is an example of such a concept; it is also an example of how difficult it is to turn even a simple urban design idea into reality.

The garage was a project of the Department of Traffic, with the plans drawn up under the supervision of the Department of Public Works. The garage had been floating about in the city's Capital Improvement Plan for many years without any mention of truck docks, so using the garage site for this purpose required the agreement of the city's budget bureau, and then the approval of a Capital Budget Amendment by the Planning Commission and the city legislature, the Board of Estimate. Then came the question: How do you separate the capital costs of the truck docks and the garage, when each is to be financed in a different way? In the end, to simplify things somewhat, the garage was done as a "turn-key" project for a lump sum by a private developer. Next, there were all the legal questions involved in connecting the garage to the stores, agreeing on appropriate charges, and so forth. It took a city development office at least one man-day a week for the best part of two years to see the garage–truck dock project through to a satisfactory resolution. Before the downtown Brooklyn plan is completed, it will be necessary to go through the same thing three times more, and there is no reason to assume that it will get any easier the second or third time. Downtown Brooklyn does provide, however, one of the few examples of city design where truck servicing has been accommodated on a systematic basis.

Environmental considerations are also coming to affect traffic, servicing, and parking systems, with many cities being required to produce a timetable for meeting federal air pollution standards in congested central areas. Environmental regulations could put a ceiling on

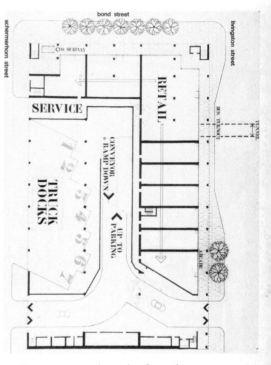

To remove truck service from the immediate vicinity of shopping, the 1969 downtown Brooklyn development plan called for incorporating truck docks for the stores in new parking garages and connecting the docks to the stores by service tunnels. This plan is gradually being carried out, but the administrative difficulties in implementing the idea are astonishing. The floor plan is the first of the Brooklyn garages to be built.

the number of self-propelled vehicles being admitted into city centers, although few practical effects of such environmental regulation have been seen to date.

When it is necessary to build either a major new expressway or a new rail–rapid transit line through an existing city, we have learned that it is necessary to assimilate it into the surrounding land-use pattern, both in order to get full value from the investment and to preserve existing activities that are important to the future of the city.

Public officials charged with building highways have traditionally kept very closely to that single purpose. They have seen themselves as road-builders, who should do their jobs as efficiently as possible. Efficiency has not included a concern for the economic and social consequences of highway construction; cost and benefit have been evaluated only on the basis of numbers of vehicles that can move from point to point.

It is well known that highways have a tremendous economic impact upon the areas in which they are built. The effect in urban areas is often negative, disrupting businesses and blighting neighborhoods. In less densely settled areas, new highways are a substantial economic stimulus: land around interchanges increases enormously in value, and whole new districts are opened up to intensive real estate development. One sometimes hears of public officials making money illegally by buying land along highway routes that they have learned about through inside information, but governments have not used these land development side effects as an instrument of public policy.

The entire Interstate system was laid out to tie together existing population centers, and no attention was given to the new development that the highways were certain to stimulate.

Nor did the original planners of the Interstate system consider that there should be any significant difference between a highway rolling through open countryside, and one cutting through a city; and remedial measures to correct the effect of highways on the city have not been part of highway plans.

It was not until the Federal Highway Act of 1970

ELEMENTS OF A DESIGN AND DEVELOPMENT STRATEGY

that there were strong legal requirements for planning highways in conjunction with other development. In addition, the Federal Clean Air Act of 1970 and the requirement for Environmental Impact Statements in the National Environmental Policy Act of 1969 provide some leverage to make the highway establishment change its ways.

The result has been the increasing use of joint development: the planning of a highway jointly with new buildings and other changes in environment and land use along the right of way.

From what once appeared to be a relatively straightforward engineering problem, highway design has become a complex, multi-disciplinary enterprise, involving an awesome variety of specialists, many different governmental agencies at federal, state, and local levels, and the participation of community groups all along the right of way.

The Westway project, between the Battery and West 42nd Street in New York City, is the joint development project that is both the most ambitious in scope and has come the nearest so far to being actually carried out. The project consists of a new West Side Highway,

Joint Development

Section at Bank Street

Southbound Highway · Vent · Northbound Highway · Proposed Street · Rebuilt West St. · Westpath

which will be placed in such a way that its construction creates new land that can be used for housing, parks, and industry.

Preliminary estimates for the cost of building the West Side Highway are so high that the highway would not be considered practicable except for the value that can be ascribed to the land created by landfill, or decking. However, the joint development proposals being studied for the West Side Highway development corri-

Section through the Westway development showing how the highway runs in a tube at the pierhead line, helping to create new buildable land between the highway and the former edge of the Hudson River.

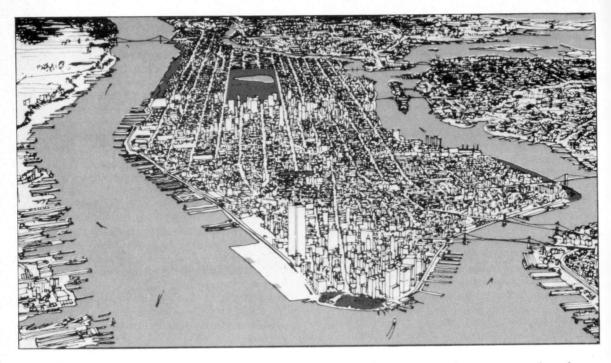

Aerial perspectives show the existing Hudson River waterfront in New York City and the proposed Westway development. A highway will be built, largely in a subsurface tube at the pierhead line, and the land above the highway and inboard of the pierhead line will be available for development as parkland, housing, or for other land uses.

dor require expenditures many times greater than for the highway itself. If the highway is to be generator of a new transit system, thousands of units of new housing, new parks, and so on, a way has to be found to fund these projects on something like the same time schedule as the highway itself.

Joint development also requires increased construction costs to meet federal environmental standards, which set stringent noise and pollution standards for development in highway corridors. Long sections of the highway will probably have to be decked over and artificially ventilated.

Joint development is a device for overcoming the defects of urban planning by single-purpose agencies, but the governmental context is still a series of programs each administered by an agency devoted to that single purpose.

At this time there seems to be no alternative to joint development as the means of building urban highways; but no one has yet made joint development work.

Somewhat better success has been achieved in relat-

ELEMENTS OF A DESIGN AND DEVELOPMENT STRATEGY

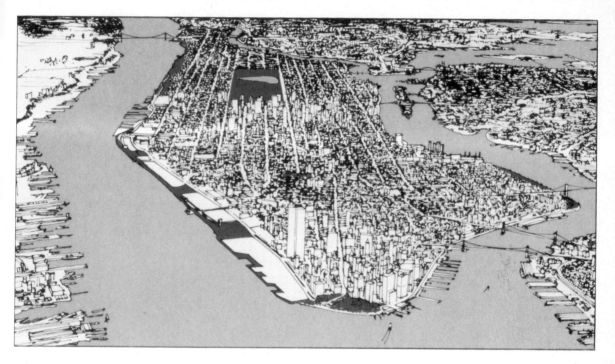

ing new rapid transit stations to surrounding development, as at Peachtree Center in Atlanta, on Market Street in San Francisco, or at the new main station of the underground light rail distributor in downtown Pittsburgh.

In general, however, while transportation systems are clearly one of the most powerful means of changing the design of the city, we have not yet invented the institutions to make such changes purposive rather than accidental. And we are only beginning to find the ways to clean up after the mistakes of earlier planning, which put traffic flow first and the form of the city second.

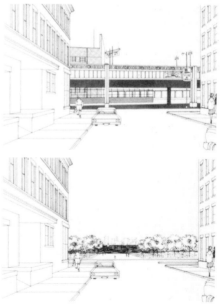

"Before" and "after" views show how a subsurface highway will open out views to the Hudson that had been blocked by the old, elevated West Side Highway.

ELEMENTS OF A DESIGN AND DEVELOPMENT STRATEGY

14

Legislative Standards
for Urban Design

Victor Bisharat, an architect who has designed many of the new buildings that have transformed the skyline of Stamford, Connecticut, was quoted by *The New York Times* as saying: "I hate how it all looks. I try to block it out of my mind. I even look the other way when I go by on the highway. I had the greatest opportunity in the world and I failed."*

Designing individual buildings, one at a time, is not at all the same thing as designing a city. Even selected examples of great architecture do not necessarily look well together as a group. This point was brought home to me when I stopped by the office of a friend who teaches an introductory course at an architectural school. He had assigned his students the job of building scale models of some of the most famous houses in the world, and there they all were sitting in rows on his desk. It looked like a scale-model slum. Frank Lloyd Wright's Robie House does not look well next to Jefferson's Monticello. Real-life examples of something like the same phenomenon can be found in New Haven, Connecticut, and Columbus, Indiana. In both places special circumstances have created a collection of fine modern buildings, and in both cases the result as city design is a good deal less than the sum of its parts.

Before the tall building, it was easier to put cities together. Baron Haussmann could take it for granted that buildings would be no higher than the extreme

*See "The 'Stamford Lesson' Influences Architecture," by Andree Brooks. *New York Times* (Real Estate Section), October 19, 1980.

A glimpse of part of the downtown Stamford, Connecticut, skyline. One of the prominent local architects has commented: "I hate how it all looks." Designing a city is not at all the same thing as designing a building.

213

1. The design of any large office tower(s) in the Market-Stanwix development should take into account design relationships with the United States Steel Building, with the projected development on the Grant Street East and County sites (to the extent that information is available at the time of design), with the buildings of Gateway Center, and with the downtown skyline in general; and these design relationships should be harmoniously resolved.

2. Any office tower(s) should be designed in such a way as to block as little sunlight as possible from public open spaces such as Market Square and the plaza of the Gateway Center.

3. Any office tower(s) should be designed in such a way that existing view corridors into and out of downtown are not blocked.

4. The design relationships between new development on the Market-Stanwix site and nearby buildings should be managed in such a way as to minimize abrupt changes in scale.

5. The elements of the Market-Stanwix development that front on Market Square should complete the enclosure of the square and be comparable in height, scale, and character to existing buildings fronting on the square.

6. The design of the Market-Stanwix project should provide a transition, through appropriate public spaces, between the plaza level of Gateway Center and Market Square, and it should, in general, provide a transition between Gateway Center's plaza-level environment and the building-street relationships prevailing elsewhere in the Golden Triangle.

7. The design of this project should take into account relationships with land uses in the surrounding blocks. Where land uses may change in the future, reference should be made to the city's downtown development strategy.

8. The design of the Market-Stanwix project should meet the individual district criteria for C5-A districts as outlined in the city planning commission's criteria for site plan review.

9. The parking provided, and truck and automobile access to the site, should be consonant with the city's traffic systems management proposals and its downtown parking plan.

10. Facilities for off-street truck loading and unloading should be provided.

11. Pleasant, weather-protected areas for bus stops should be provided according to configurations acceptable to the Port Authority

distance that people would walk upstairs. If buildings were all going to be about the same size and shape, the number of potential combinations was limited, and a series of simple regulations was enough to produce an ensemble. The success of Washington, D.C., as urban design is due as much to that city's height limitation as it is to Major L'Enfant's plan. A Washington street may be lined with a diverse collection of not very good new office buildings, but the height limitation pulls them together and gives them force as city design.

In a suburban district with quarter-acre lots or larger, assuming that the development is restricted to single-family houses of approximately the same size, the landscaping will eventually create an ensemble. Some of the most successful examples of area design in the United States are these kinds of suburbs. A single tall apartment house, however, is enough to ruin the composition.

In a downtown full of tall buildings, or a dense residential neighborhood where it is the buildings that make the environment, each new structure ought to be sensitively adjusted to its context; and, ideally, there ought to be some kind of overall design concept. Many architects understand these issues very well, although some of the best recent designers of individual buildings have been relatively indifferent to matters of context and ensemble. But there is often a conflict of interest between what is best for an individual owner and the interests of the community in a better urban design. As the architect is working for the individual owner, it is not surprising that the interests of the community often take second place.

An example of such a potential conflict of interest came up in Pittsburgh during the design of the new corporate headquarters for PPG Industries. The main office tower of this headquarters was to be located just to the south of a public park called Market Square. The rental agents for the building suggested a floor plan and placement for the tower which would have put it directly south of the square and of such a size and shape that it would have blocked all sunlight from the square during the hours between twelve and two in the after-

and in locations that accord with the downtown development strategy's bus route plan.

12. The design of the Market-Stanwix project should meet the circulation criteria set forth in the city planning department's criteria for site plan review.

13. Bridges over streets should not create cavernous spaces that are unpleasant and unsafe for pedestrians.

14. If the retail segment of the city's downtown development strategy should indicate that a department store would be desirable as part of the Market-Stanwix development, an appropriate site should be provided.

Part of the standards for site plan review given by the city to PPG before design of the building began.

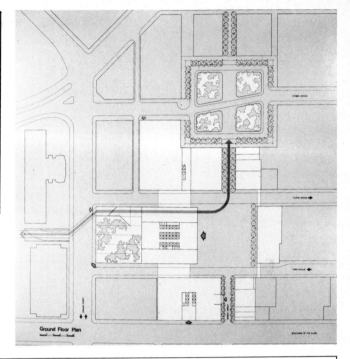

Ground Floor Plan

Perspective and site plan of the PPG Industries complex.

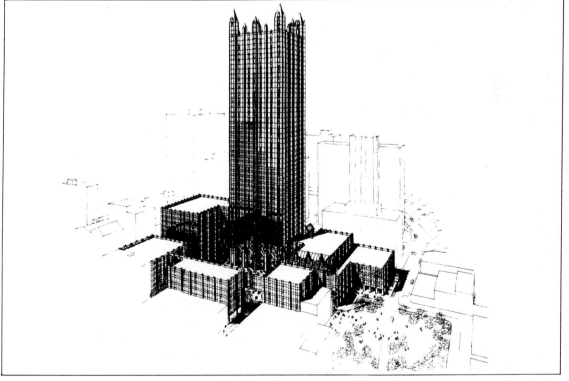

noon, precisely the time when the square is most popular with nearby office workers. The city of Pittsburgh had suggested that sunlight on the square should be one of the building's design criteria in its urban design guidelines. In ordinary circumstances, one would expect the need to create "the most rentable floor plan" to win out over the people eating lunch in the park. In this case, the architect was Philip Johnson, who has enough prestige and persuasiveness to overcome a presentation by a national real estate firm. He gave the tower a different shape and moved it to the west, away from the square.

Johnson asserts that he never bothered to read the city's urban design guidelines but was pursuing a design concept of his own. The point of this anecdote, however, is that someone has to look after the public interest in these situations. Sometimes the architect may be able to do it, but often the architect must give in and solve the immediate problems of the client. It is left to local government to look after the public's need for urban design. There are several different mechanisms for doing so; we have already looked at special zoning districts in Chapters 6 and 7. Before considering mechanisms, however, we ought to list the most important issues that are likely to come up.

The first category of issues concerns land-use policy. Preserving a district of legitimate theaters would be an example; other such issues include preserving the continuity of retail frontages, preventing retail uses being replaced entirely by banks and ticket offices, or ensuring that a portion of a commercial development be devoted to housing. While people generally describe such questions as land-use issues, they are also matters of city design: the functional arrangement of the city.

Another category of issues concerns the perception of the city skyline from a distance, one of the Stamford, Connecticut, problems. There is the question of where tall buildings should be permitted. Within tall building districts, the geometrical relationships among towers, and the way new buildings are perceived from significant vantage points, are important design issues. In Boston, Massachusetts, there was an evident failure to

Looking After the Public's Interest in Building Design

ELEMENTS OF A DESIGN AND DEVELOPMENT STRATEGY

think along these lines, which resulted in the intrusion of a new government office tower into the traditional picture postcard view of the Statehouse dome ("The Hub of the Universe") as seen from Boston Common.

Then there are all the design issues that concern the relationship between a new building and its present or future neighbors. There are all the traditional light and air questions, such as the problem of noontime sunlight on Market Square in Pittsburgh. The ability of a building to receive direct sunlight has taken on a new significance now that individual solar-powered systems are being developed for buildings. Preservation of view corridors into and out of city districts is important. Often when urban renewal projects have removed streets, new buildings have ended up blocking important views of rivers and harbors, or of the surrounding countryside.

Relationships of height, scale, materials, and architectural character are each important, particularly when a new building is part of a historic district, or is located close to one.

The functional connections to surrounding buildings are a major force in city design. The relationships among public spaces include concourse and overhead bridge connections as well as arcades, plazas, and indoor public spaces. Connections to rapid transit, from parking to offices, hotels, and retail uses, and among various retail areas, can make all the difference to a smoothly functioning downtown or regional center. How these connections are designed is also important. The experience can be like threading a maze, or of a well-managed sequence of pleasant and interesting spaces, depending on the skill of the architects and the consistency of the urban design policies. As mentioned before, Market Street in San Francisco is a place where these connections have been well managed, as is Peachtree Center in Atlanta, and the relationship between the interior court of the IDS Building in Minneapolis and that city's Skyway system. There is no need (and no room) to list all the examples where such connections have not been well managed.

We should also add to our list urban design issues relating to transportation and circulation. Some of

Model photographs of the PPG World Industries headquarters in Pittsburgh, designed by Philip Johnson & John Burgee.

them are as mundane as the placement of truck docks, which, for example, should not occur on a shopping street. The provision of sheltered spaces for people to wait for buses is an urban design issue, particularly where buses are the primary means of rapid transit. The number of parking places permitted relates to overall downtown parking and circulation policies. The number and location of entrances and exits to parking garages also affect city design. This is a set of issues that is well understood by the public. Most people have had the experience of being trapped by traffic waiting for a line of cars to go into or come out of a garage. What people probably don't realize is that this is a city design problem. It reveals a lack of thoughtful planning in the same way that, when you open a door and it bangs into another open door, you discover a lack of thoughtful planning on the part of the architect or builder.

If this is a representative list of urban design issues, how can a locality go about dealing with them through legislation? One method is the special district, described in detail in Chapter 6. Another method is design review. The developer presents the proposed building to the planning authorities. It is then reviewed by staff, usually including urban designers, and changes may be suggested before the building is approved. The perils of negotiated zoning have been discussed in Chapter 7. There are also architectural perils from the design review process, which result from the way the process is organized in most architects' offices. The person who brings the drawings to show to the planning authorities is seldom the one who actually designed the building. Either the architect is too eminent to attend such meetings, or the design takes place in a special design department, and the project manager who deals with the authorities may have only a very sketchy idea of what was going through the designer's mind when certain decisions were made:

PROJECT MANAGER: Everything's fine; we've all agreed. The only thing is, you'll have to move the building back ten feet.

ELEMENTS OF A DESIGN AND DEVELOPMENT STRATEGY

DESIGNER: But we can't do that. Don't you remember there's a utility easement right behind the building?

PROJECT MANAGER: Well, you'll have to work it out somehow. If I go back and try to change things now, the whole agreement will unravel.

Obviously, changing the design to meet such an arbitrarily imposed constraint is no way to create good architecture. When you also consider that design review usually occurs at a late stage in the design process when making changes is both difficult and expensive, you can see why the results of the review often satisfy nobody.

Pittsburgh has a discretionary site plan review provision in its zoning ordinance that makes each building subject to this kind of discretionary evaluation. One method that has been developed to improve the process is for the Planning Commission to adopt a set of standards for site plan review for important sites *before* the building is designed. These standards are written in performance language, so as not to prejudge the solution to the design problems. The standards then provide a checklist for evaluating the design, and should ensure that major design issues are not brought up for the first time at a late stage of the design process. For example, one of the items on the list of standards for the PPG World Industries headquarters in downtown Pittsburgh was the following: "Any office tower(s) should be designed in such a way as to block as little sunlight as possible from public open spaces such as Market Square and the plaza of Gateway Center." To be sure, in this instance the architect claims to have thrown the criteria away without reading them. However, when it was time to evaluate the building, it proved to have met all the requirements.

In another downtown Pittsburgh situation where the designs for a building did not, at first, seem to be meeting the guidelines at all, it became a matter not of the taste of staff urban designers versus a nationally known architectural firm and a large and powerful company, but of an adopted city policy that was not being fol-

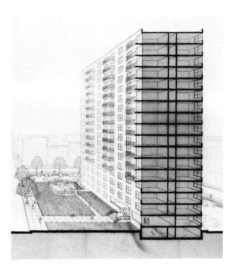

A conventional New York City apartment house for an R-8 zone takes a form virtually dictated by the zoning.

The housing quality alternative regulations permit buildings such as this one, which would not be possible under the older regulations.

New York City's Housing Quality Regulations

NEIGHBORHOOD IMPACT	MAXIMUM VALUE Built Up	Non Built Up
1. Street wall setback*	4.55	n.a.**
2. Sunlight in open space*	3.60	4.70
3. Length of street wall*	3.60	7.55
4. Shadow on buildings*	3.05	5.40
5. Height of street wall*	3.05	n.a.
6. Street trees*	2.85	4.15
7. Height of building*	2.15	n.a.
8. Transparency ratio at ground floor*	2.15	3.20
	25.00	25.00

RECREATION SPACE	
1. Type and size*	8.50
2. Winter sun	5.00
3. Landscaping	2.75
4. Covered parking	2.65
5. Visibility of parking*	2.65
6. Trees*	2.45
7. Seating	1.00
	25.00

SECURITY AND SAFETY	
1. Vis. from public space to elevator door or general circulation stair	3.90
2. Vis. of priv. outdoor space from lobby*	3.90
3. Surveillance from large apartments	3.30
4. No. of apts. serviced by lobby	2.90
5. Vis. of parking from exit point*	2.25
6. Vis. of parking area from lobby	2.20
7. Distance from elevator to apt.*	1.85
8. Road separation*	1.80
9. Vis. from elevator door or general circulation stair to apartment door*	1.80
10. Visibility of mail room	1.10
	25.00

APARTMENTS	
1. Size of apartment*	3.75
2. Sunlight in apartment*	3.20
3. Window size*	3.20
4. Visual privacy--apt. to apt.*	3.20
5. Visual privacy--street to apt.	1.75
6. Balconies	1.70
7. Daylight in hallways	1.50
8. Distance from parking to garage exit*	1.50
9. Daylight in kitchen	1.50
10. Pram and bicycle storage	1.30
11. Waste storage facilities*	1.20
12. Garbage pickup facilities	1.20
	25.00

*Minimum compliance levels established

**n.a.--not applicable

The housing quality regulations seek to create objective values for good design by providing a list of possible housing quality points that a developer could obtain, and which would permit development at the maximum density.

Drawings illustrate examples of housing quality criteria in the security and safety category.

lowed. That was what made the difference, and ensured a reasonable result.

New York City's Standards for Planned Unit Development, mentioned on page 68, are another example of an attempt to articulate standards for a discretionary design review process before the architect goes to work.

There is another New York City example, which tries to introduce the flexibility of design review into a set of procedures that can be legislated "as of right"—the housing quality legislation. This legislation sought to objectify what constitutes good design, particularly as an antidote to the design biases of New York City's Comprehensive Zoning Revision of 1961, which had a built-in prejudice in favor of towers surrounded by open space. The provisions creating these towers were introduced as a corrective to the dark courts and light wells that characterized the old, 1916 zoning; changes gave rise to new problems, particularly in residential areas.

The minimum standards written into the zoning became the specification of a new residential building type: a tower that was two or three times as tall as the neighboring buildings, surrounded by open space that was seldom pleasant, often dangerous, and, in low-density districts, almost invariably filled with parked cars. The open areas break the continuity of the street facade, and the tall towers frequently throw nearby buildings into shade for much of the day. The zoning takes little account of differences in neighborhood and changes in topography; and, because of the restrictive nature of the regulations, the same stereotypes are repeated all over the city.

These new apartment towers have become very unpopular, a prime cause of the community resistance to new building projects encountered almost everywhere in New York. Not only do the neighbors object; so do the tenants. People are beginning to suspect that the tall building is not a suitable type of apartment house for anyone but the well-to-do, who can afford doormen, elevator attendants, and the service staff necessary to keep the building secure and well maintained. It also helps if the tenants can afford to escape to the country on weekends.

ELEMENTS OF A DESIGN AND DEVELOPMENT STRATEGY

Tall apartment houses are not always popular with developers either. It is true that high floors command premium rents, at least until the building is surrounded by other towers. But this kind of high-rise building, with its relatively small floors, is very expensive to build; and the open-space and setback regulations are so restrictive that many developers have found themselves stuck with sites that could have been developed under the old regulations, but don't seem to be an economic proposition under the new law.

One solution, much advocated by developers, is to increase the zoned density all over New York City. This move would make building more profitable for the developer, until the land prices had risen to take account of the change. All the other criticized factors of the 1961 zoning would simply be made even less acceptable.

If there is to be no increase in density, it is not possible to use new incentive provisions similar to those for plazas or covered pedestrian spaces, or like those in use in the special districts.

Instead, the legislation has accepted the existing residential zones and their mapped density as being based on sound planning principles, but suggests scrapping all the technical aspects of residential zoning controls that are not mandated by other sets of regulations, like the Building Code and the Multiple Dwelling Law.

In place of setback lines or open-space ratios, the developer, and the architect, would elect to include certain design elements in their building from a list specified in a comprehensive zoning amendment. The use of these elements would be rewarded by a point system also specified in the law. A building that had a high enough score on this scale of quality points would be permitted to attain the highest floor area scheduled for that particular zoning district. Buildings whose design received a lower score would be proportionately smaller.

There are more possible quality design elements than any one building would be expected to include, thus recognizing that design is always a series of choices—that circumstances alter cases, and you can't win 'em

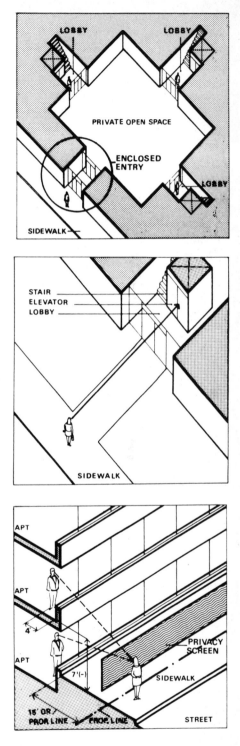

all. Sometimes one objective can be achieved only at the expense of another. The architect can choose appropriate design elements in relation to the existing neighborhood, the shape of the site, the topography, and so forth, instead of adapting the needs of his client to a single rigid stereotype.

The new law has delineated four categories of elements that are rewarded with points for design quality: they respond to criteria for neighborhood impact, recreation space, security and safety, and apartment design. The scoring system is set up in such a way that the developer must achieve a minimum distribution of points among the four categories. A list of all the criteria, and some representative examples, are shown on pages 220–221.

The whole design quality system is the product of an exhaustive, two-year study that included the question of building costs. It is expected that the developer will be able to balance increased costs caused by some of the elements selected, by savings created in not having to comply with some of the old regulations, and by the increased feasibility of building on many sites that were not economic before.

The new regulations can be administered in the same way as conventional zoning, the provisions being made available by right, subject to approval by the Building Department. There would be no discretionary rulings by the Planning Commission and no individual special permits with their attendant public hearings. However, at the present time, New York City has adopted these regulations only as a special permit procedure.

The effect of this zoning amendment is to bring the benefits of urban design policies to neighborhoods that are neither part of high-intensity business districts nor in need of extensive urban renewal. It is also a principle capable of considerable extension and further development.

ELEMENTS OF A DESIGN AND DEVELOPMENT STRATEGY

15

A Public Investment Strategy

We all know that cities are short of money, and cannot afford to do everything that is necessary. At the same time, local governments spend large sums on capital projects that help determine the overall design of the city, and have the powers to enhance the feasibility of private development through various kinds of subsidies or by direct public investment.

If public investment policies are viewed strategically, as a means of carrying out urban design objectives as well as providing the solution to immediate problems, the design of the city can be greatly enhanced.

Let us first consider the city's building program, the police and fire stations, the schools and community centers, garages, hospitals and clinics, and the various subsidized housing programs.

This enormous amount of capital construction has, more often than not, represented a wasted opportunity. The immediate needs of the locality were served relatively successfully, but the overall design of the city and the general standard of architecture have not been supported as they should have been.

The problem of quality in municipal architecture is frequently discussed in terms of architect selection; but the choice of architectural firm, while it is obviously significant, is not the whole story. The context in which the architect must work is equally important. In fact, architectural quality, or the lack of it, is the product of

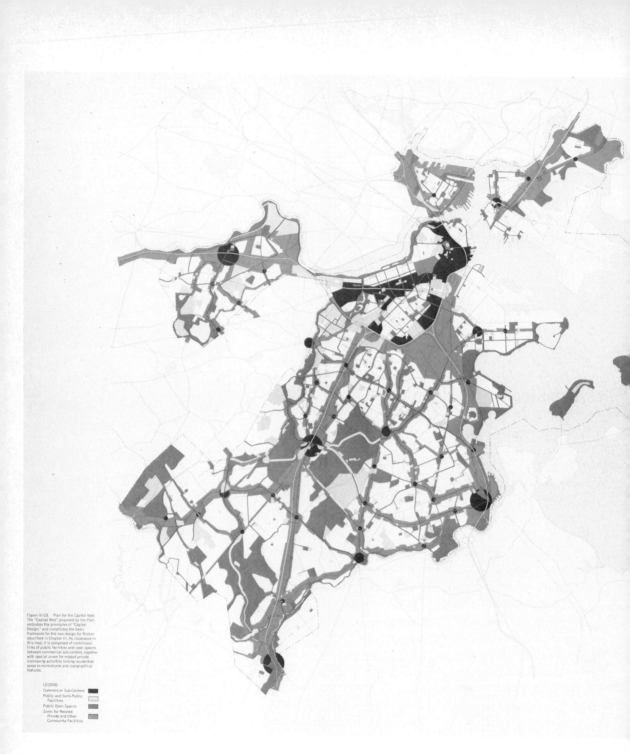

Figure III-23. Plan for the Capital Web.
The "Capital Web" proposed by the Plan
embodies the principles of "Capital
Design," and constitutes the basic
framework for the new design for Boston
described in Chapter III. As illustrated in
this map, it is composed of continuous
links of public facilities and open spaces
between commercial sub-centers, together
with special zones for related private
community activities linking residential
areas to recreational and topographical
features.

LEGEND
Commercial Sub-Centers
Public and Semi-Public
    Facilities
Public Open Spaces
Zones for Related
    Private and Other
    Community Facilities

ELEMENTS OF A DESIGN AND DEVELOPMENT STRATEGY

a system that includes the selection of the site, the budget, the program, the architect, and the staff of the agency that reviews the architect's work. A real increase in the architectural quality and design significance of a city's building program requires a revision of the whole system, otherwise efforts at reform will produce only a few token, or "showcase," buildings that are given special treatment by top-level staff.

There are sections of many cities where a great deal of public money has been invested over time. If you stand at an intersection in the middle of one of these districts and look around you, everything you see may be the product of a public construction program. On one corner is a publicly aided housing project. On another corner is a school. The third corner has a health clinic, the fourth another publicly aided housing project, this time for the elderly. Down the block is a new police station, another block away there is a fire station. Each project has been designed and constructed without any reference to the others: as so often happens in cities, the whole is a great deal less than the sum of its parts.

The problem here rests with the city's site selection process, which is directed toward the needs of the various agencies and programs rather than toward localities. The problems of each functional area—housing, education, police, and so on—are considered separately; and this separation is expressed in the resulting city development. It is true that site selection for publicly aided construction has been considered systematically in a few cities. A concept of a "capital web" of government construction was articulated in the 1965 General Plan for the city of Boston. This concept was in turn the outgrowth of the experience of the director of the Boston Redevelopment Authority, Edward J. Logue, when he had been director of redevelopment in New Haven, Connecticut. Logue had worked out a method of using New Haven's public investments, which were scheduled to take place in any event, as the 25 percent "local share" required by federal urban renewal legislation. He was thus able to generate an

Opposite: a map illustrating the "capital web" concept developed in the 1965–75 General Plan for the city of Boston. Commercial subcenters are linked by continuous public facilities and open spaces, giving control of the public environment. Residential neighborhoods fill in the sectors in between.

The "Capital Web"

Opposite: site plan of housing in Minneapolis, showing its relationship to Loring Greenway. More information about the Loring Park Extension and this housing can be found in Chapter 10. Architects are Frederick Bentz/Milo Thompson & Associates, Inc.

New downtown housing in Minneapolis has been developed along the Loring Park Extension, a public investment paid for by tax-increment financing.

unusually large amount of federal investment in New Haven, by using the local capital projects as "leverage."

This experience was developed by Boston's planning director of the time, David Crane, into a theory of the capital web, in which public investment became the framework for controlling the location and timing of all investment in an area. Site selection in most cities, however, is still a haphazard process too much of the time. The significance of capital investment is seldom clearly understood, except in rapidly developing suburbs, where the street and utility system determine what areas can develop.

There is another aspect to site selection that also works against good urban design: the set of standards articulated by the individual agencies. A Board of Education might supply figures showing how large a site is required by an elementary school with a certain number of seats and a playground of appropriate size. What is not stated is that this calculation is based on certain assumptions about the building. The site can accommodate the classrooms if the building is two stories high; there is room for the playground if the auditorium is kept to the edge of the site. In other words, the basic design of the building is frequently set (or the design possibilities severely restricted) at the same time the site is selected, which is usually long before the architect becomes involved. There are even more subtle preconceptions that affect city design and are embodied in seemingly reasonable standards articulated by single-purpose authorities. For example, for years the New York City Board of Education refused to accept the concept that an elementary school gymnasium could also be used as a cafeteria and as an auditorium. As a result, the minimum number of seats for an elementary school became larger, in order to spread the costs of an additional large room or rooms. The large number of seats made for fewer, bigger schools, which in turn made it more difficult to integrate the design of elementary schools with the housing in a local neighborhood.

Similar tacit assumptions are made in determining the budget allocation for a building. The budget is usually based on the cost of comparable buildings already

ELEMENTS OF A DESIGN AND DEVELOPMENT STRATEGY

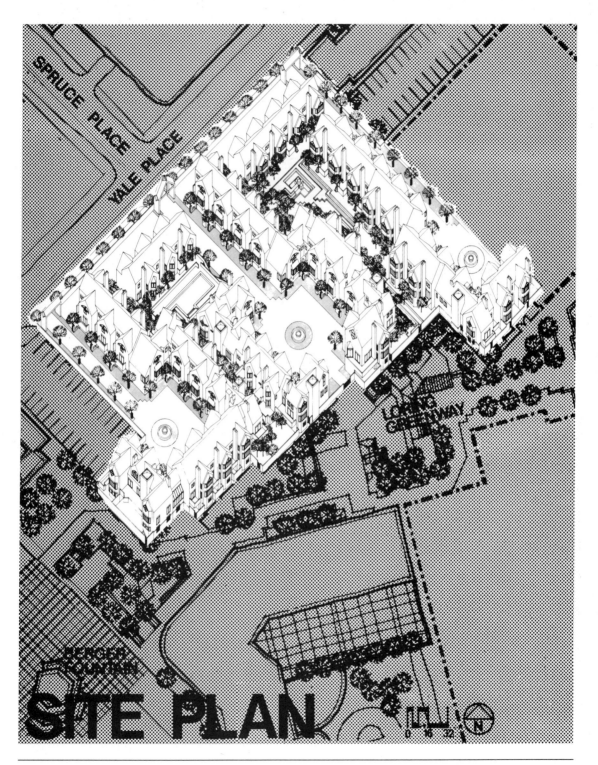

SPRUCE PLACE

YALE PLACE

LORING GREENWAY

BERGER FOUNTAIN

SITE PLAN

0 8 22

N

completed, plus, perhaps, an allowance for rising construction costs. Such a budgeting system discourages innovation unless it can be readily seen that the change will cost the same or less than the system on which the budget is based. There is no built-in method of assessing the benefits to be gained from any cost increase (to permit greater flexibility of design needed to make use of an unorthodox site, let us say) or even of accepting the risk of delay that might result from sending an unfamiliar form of construction out for bid. Again, a series of fundamental architectural decisions about layout, materials, and construction have been made well before the architect comes into the picture, and important urban design options have been foreclosed.

The illustrations here and on page 229 show the integration of an elementary school into the housing at Roosevelt Island in New York City, proving what can be done when this kind of possibility is considered before either the school or the housing is planned or designed. Roosevelt Island was developed by the New York State Urban Development Corporation, whose president at the time was Edward J. Logue.

Because capital budgets are understood to be important to planning the future of cities, the task of drafting a capital budget is often given to city planning departments. The problem is that, in a period of rapidly rising construction prices, no one really knows what a capital project is going to cost until the actual bids are received. As a result, capital budgets—and especially five-year capital improvement programs—have a strong element of fiction to them. A project can bounce around in a capital improvement program for years, without ever getting closer to implementation, because the real capital budget is drawn by amendment after people know what the actual costs are. Who decides how much money it is appropriate to spend on an individual capital project? Answer: budget examiners, or the staff of the agency that will construct it—public works, housing, education, or whatever—not the staff of the planning agency. As a result, while the planning agency is theoretically setting priorities, the effective capital program is often in other hands.

The school system at Roosevelt Island in New York City has been completely integrated into the design of the community. Here a school entrance fronts onto a shopping arcade.

ELEMENTS OF A DESIGN AND DEVELOPMENT STRATEGY

The crucial capital budget decision is how much money to allocate to a given project, particularly when there is nowhere near enough money to fund all the potential improvements that some group of important people wants to see built. The decision is made by the book, by a government official who knows that good performance is not laying oneself open to criticism. If a building looks precisely like one that was built five years ago, any construction cost increase must be the result of inflation. If the building looks different, even if it might cost less than repeating the same building, the official is open to criticism. If it really does cost

The Blackwell School on Roosevelt Island, within a courtyard formed by apartment houses. As the neighborhood is racially integrated, no busing is needed. Usually public investments in schools and subsidized housing are considered separately, so that such pleasant—and obvious—physical relationships are not possible. The architects for the buildings are Sert, Jackson Associates.

Urban Design by the Book

more, the official has no basis for approving it just because some architect or member of an urban design staff asserted that it represented superior design.

If the decision must be made by the book, the only answer is to change the book. The standards for street lighting and graphics illustrated in Chapter 12 represent such a change in the book. An official can approve the expenditure because the particular specification has been adopted as city policy; there is no need to look for cheaper alternatives. It is possible, although difficult, to write a similar book for schools, housing, police, fire stations, and so on, and even to write urban design procedures into site selection and building standards. Until cities rewrite their books on capital expenditure, they will not be getting their money's worth in city design, although individual structures may appear to be economical. It is true that no rule book is as good as really imaginative case-by-case decisions. But it is much more plausible to imagine a good rule book that is amended from time to time than it is to invent an administrative procedure that can be relied upon to make good architectural and urban design decisions.

A locality's public investment strategy also includes methods of promoting private investment. A traditional means is by the strategic use of a public project. A park paid for by government enhances the real estate value of the property fronting on it. A convention center, which may operate at a loss, draws business to a city and improves the overall revenue base. A parking garage with rates that barely pay back costs is an unattractive private investment, but a sound one for a city that is promoting downtown shopping and offices.

Three Methods of Direct Public Investment in Private Projects

There are also ways to use public investment as a direct aid to private projects. There are three traditional methods: direct capital grants, interest subsidies, and tax abatement. A fourth method, rent supplements for individual families, is really a social welfare program. It can be used to promote development by tying the aid to apartments in a particular building. The chapter and verse of all of these methods varies as legislation is amended and replaced. In the old days of federally aided urban renewal, capital grants took the form of

ELEMENTS OF A DESIGN AND DEVELOPMENT STRATEGY

land write-down, a subsidy that permitted localities to buy expensive land, clear it, and offer it for development at an attractive price. The "Feds" made up the loss. Today, a popular federal program is the Department of Housing and Urban Development's Urban Development Action Grant, or UDAG. Localities are discouraged from using UDAGs for land write-down. Instead, they are urged to apply for private projects that are well along in planning, and require a relatively small boost to make them feasible. These projects must be attractive to private investment, and, at the same time, be seen to offer immediate help to the poor people of the area. You can imagine that people capable of writing a successful UDAG application are in great demand. They must describe a project that is only feasible with the grant, but which some private investor has spent a great deal of time bringing to the point where the project can go ahead quickly once funding is received. It must be a sound investment that will receive conventional private financing; but the poor must benefit. In practice, many UDAGs seem to be second mortgages on downtown hotels. Hotels are good for the tax base; they also employ a lot of maids and dishwashers, which in a way is an aid to the poor. A UDAG second mortgage has the additional attraction of being a loan, which the locality will eventually get back. No doubt the development community will have only just adapted to the subtleties of the UDAG program when it will be replaced, or given a new set of administrative standards.

Another form of direct capital subsidy is the Community Development Grant, which is a means of revenue sharing. The federal government transmits this money to a locality, which can then spend it as it sees fit, within general guidelines. Many people see this as a more efficient concept than the categorical grants like UDAGs. Community development money has a way of finding its way into a city's normal capital budget where it is subject to the normal competitive pressures. Instead of borrowing capital money with bonds, the locality receives federal money, which in a sense is borrowed, if it is part of an annual budget running a deficit.

Localities can borrow money in the municipal bond market at lower rates than those prevailing for private obligations because the interest from municipal bonds is exempt from federal taxes, and from local taxes in the state issuing the bond. A locality can transfer this lower rate of interest to a private project by borrowing on its behalf. Usually these obligations are revenue bonds; that is, the bond is backed by the projected revenues of the project itself, rather than by the full faith and credit of the municipality. An industrial development bond issue is backed by the projected payments of the industry that will occupy the factory to be built with the proceeds of the bonds. If that industry should default, the bondholders lose. Interest rates for revenue bonds are thus higher than for full-faith-and-credit bonds, which are based on the city's taxing power, but are still lower than the industry would have to pay in the private bond market. In this way, an industry can be encouraged to locate in a city's industrial park, providing jobs for local residents, rather than building in another city, or in an unincorporated rural area. Municipal bonds are often used to finance limited-profit housing projects, to provide a parking garage as part of a larger project, and to further other development objectives that are seen to be in the public interest.

A popular program right now is for localities to borrow money in the municipal bond market, then turn around and lend this money to private homeowners and small businesses to promote local improvement districts. The recipient gets a loan at a lower rate of interest than would be charged by a bank, often in a district where banks are reluctant to lend. The locality can charge slightly more than the rate it is paying, thus covering its administrative costs. An attractive program; although what you think of its fiscal soundness depends on your perception of the future of urban neighborhoods.

Tax Abatement

Tax abatement is another attractive program. It doesn't seem to cost localities anything, because it is usually offered to projects on sites that are paying little or nothing in the way of taxes. Offering a graduated real

THE ELEMENTS OF A DESIGN AND DEVELOPMENT STRATEGY

estate tax-abatement schedule—0 the first year up to full payment in the tenth year is a common formula—will help make a new development feasible; and eventually that project will enhance the locality's tax base. What you think of the fiscal soundness of tax abatement depends on whether you believe it is increasing development or not. If the effect of the program is simply to move development from sites where full taxes would be paid to sites where they are not, the economics of the move must be of real importance or the locality is the loser. On the other hand, if development is generated, the locality wins. Tax abatement could be used to further specific urban design objectives, particularly in cities where zoning incentives are meaningless. The city of Boston studied a Tremont Street Special District, which was not enacted, where part of the incentive system included tax benefits for the retention and rehabilitation of existing buildings.

Tax abatement has been used extensively in Manhattan to promote housing rehabilitation and the conversion of loft buildings to apartments. The trade-off is that apartments in these buildings are subject to restrictions on future rent increases. Some people argue that, once the program is understood by the real estate market, land and building prices adjust to take it into account. The prices rise, and development is only feasible with the abatement.

The basic problem with tax abatement is the where-will-it-all-end syndrome. Localities have little revenue to spare, and must consequently use tax abatement sparingly.

Another method of promoting development, tax-increment financing, combines municipal borrowing power with adjustments of the taxing power. If a public project will enhance the value of nearby properties, why not earmark the revenue increase that is attributable to that increase in value, and use it to pay for the capital costs of the project? The Loring Park Extension in Minneapolis was paid for in this way. By extending Loring Park, the municipality was creating a series of attractive sites for downtown housing. The bonds sold

Tax-Increment Financing

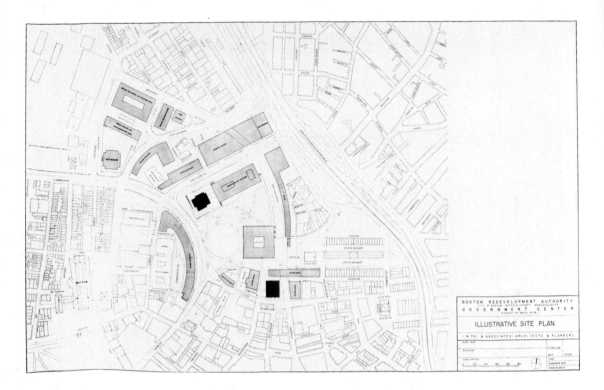

A map by I. M. Pei & Partners showing the original site plan for the Boston Government Center. A calculated public investment strategy, the concentration of public buildings was meant to catalyze a renewal of the downtown office district, which it did.

to finance building the park were backed by tax revenue from the sites fronting the park. The taxes equal to those paid before the park was built continued to go to the city's usual budgets, but the *increment* was allocated to paying for the park. Another attractive idea; but in an inflationary period when tax increases are routine, there are problems with tying tax increases to specific projects. Again, where will it all end?

Unfortunately, there is no Santa Claus. Municipal revenues will probably always be limited in comparison with municipal objectives. Because money is scarce, it should be used strategically to help promote larger public policies, including urban design. Public investment policies, which seem rational in terms of specific, limited objectives, have often proved wasteful in terms of city design and development. A public investment strategy is the means of correcting this problem.

Boston's Government Center district is an example of a public investment strategy in which buildings that

THE ELEMENTS OF A DESIGN AND DEVELOPMENT STRATEGY

were required by various government agencies were used strategically to stimulate the redevelopment of downtown Boston. The Government Center is also an example of an urban design plan that has actually been carried out in its entirety, as is demonstrated by comparing the original diagram by I. M. Pei & Partners with the completed district.

The Boston Government Center in 1978. One of the few urban designs for an American city to be carried out almost in its entirety, the plan retains its original concept despite the participation of many different architects.

Afterword:

The Urban Design Profession

What is the difference between an urban designer and an urban planner, or between an urban designer and an architect? We were forced to consider these definitions seriously in New York in 1967 because we were creating a new institution. The public employees' union and the city's personnel department required that the new urban design jobs we proposed be established under civil service regulations, with the appointments made on the basis of performance on examinations. The definitions we made then still appear to me to be valid.

A city planner, it seemed to us, was someone who was primarily concerned with the allocation of resources according to projections of future need. Allocating funds for a capital budget is a series of planning decisions, because it involves determinations of need for, as an example, a new school in a particular district, and balancing off that need against those of other areas.

Architects, on the other hand, design buildings. They prepare a set of contract documents so that the building, let us say, a school, can be constructed, and they take legal responsibility for the process.

There is a substantial middle ground between these professions, and each has some claim to it, but neither fills it very well.

Planners tend to regard land use as an allocation of resources problem, parceling out land, for zoning purposes, without much knowledge of its three-dimensional characteristics or the nature of the building that may be placed on it in the future. The result is that most zoning ordinances and official land-use plans produce stereotyped and unimaginative buildings.

Land-use planning would clearly be improved if it involved someone who understands three-dimensional design.

Good architects will do all they can to relate the buildings they design to their surroundings, but have no control over what happens off the property they have been hired to consider. As we have seen, there may well be a conflict of interest between good urban design and the needs of an architect's client, so that cities full of good modern buildings—like Columbus, Indiana, or New Haven, Connecticut—do not achieve a corresponding improvement in their overall design. Someone is needed to design the city, not just the buildings.

Urban Designers Design Cities —Not Just the Buildings

Many urban design measures are within the control of local government, so it is not surprising that a high proportion of urban design work has been commissioned by localities. Such design can be carried out by staff or by consultants, and there are advantages to both. Staff people are on hand when the real decisions are being made—when the decisionmakers have their feet up at the end of the day, and the consultants are on their way to the airport. On the other hand, consultants may have more credibility than staff, if only because they do indeed come from outside the local decision-making hierarchy, and can bring the distillation of their experiences elsewhere.

When New York City's Urban Design Group was started in 1967, there were only a handful of urban designers working for city governments. Today, people who are urban designers by title or function can be found on the staffs of planning departments, landmark commissions, redevelopment agencies, transportation authorities, and public works departments, although not necessarily in positions where they have much to say about making city policies.

In planning agencies, much of the urban designers' day-to-day work is probably concerned with design review, particularly of projects that come in under discretionary zoning provisions such as planned unit development. Urban design staff also work at community and special district planning. Designers who work for preservation agencies are likely to do a lot of design review, particularly in determining conformity to historic district regulations. They will be involved in evaluating historic buildings to determine whether they are suitable, or feasible, for preservation. Urban designers in development agencies work on area development plans, and review the drawings of individual architects to try to make the buildings conform to such development plans. There are not as many urban designers working for transportation or public works departments as there should be; but, as we have seen, there is plenty for them to do.

In 1967, there were perhaps ten consulting firms that specialized in offering urban design services. Today there are dozens, and, as it doesn't cost anything more to print "Urban Design" on a letterhead, many more engineers, architects, and planners express themselves as willing to offer such services. Unfortunately, urban design is easier said than done. There have been many urban design plans that did not take into account economic, political, and social feasibility.

There are other potential roles for urban designers in the private sector, besides working for consulting firms. As real estate development becomes more complex, putting a greater emphasis on projects with many components that will take a long time to complete, there is room for in-house urban design services within real estate development companies. Similarly, as the permanent lenders begin to take equity positions in real estate projects, there is a need for urban design review by the staffs of the insurance companies and other financial institutions that make the mortgage commitments.

What training and experience qualify someone to be an urban designer? Some kind of training in design seems to be essential—normally the most thorough is that offered by architectural schools. It can also be argued that, unless an urban designer understands how buildings are put together, urban design could just be an exercise in moving cubes around on a map. However, many landscape architecture curricula offer a good introduction to the design process, and a few planning studios do as well, so it is not appropriate to consider urban design to be simply a branch of architecture. The landscape architect in particular is likely to have a better background in regional environmental analysis than an architect would.

There are problems in using the traditional studio format to teach urban design. The studio is essentially a simulation technique. It works well enough for architecture or landscape architecture, with the teacher representing both the muse and the client; but it becomes difficult to simulate a situation that normally contains government officials, investors, and community interests. The graduate program I direct at the City College of New York gets around this problem by offering actual professional experience instead of a studio. Students work half-time in a professional or governmental office, and are paid for their work. This approach is one that can work only in a big city. A few other schools are able to offer their students real problems through a research institute or community design center run by the school.

The rest of urban design education is concerned with introducing the student to ways of thinking about and solving the problems that will be encountered in trying to design cities. These problems come under the headings of economic, political, and social feasibility, so that an urban design curriculum should introduce the student to law, public administration, real estate economics, and the research techniques of the social sciences. Our own university happens to have an excellent environmental psychology department, so I also suggest one of their courses to our students. In my view, the most important additional subject for the urban designer to understand is real estate economics. You can always hire a lawyer, or a social science researcher, but people who know how to put together real estate deals are seldom available for consultation. We also put strong emphasis on the case study method. There are a lot of examples of urban design around, and a lot of mistakes; why not try to learn from them?

Of course, despite the fragments of a designed city that can be found in various places, city design itself remains a prediction—or a presumption. In the book on our urban design experiences in New York City published in 1974, I quoted a definition of an urban designer as someone who knew the answers to a lot of questions no one was asking. Today I would say that people are asking the questions, but they don't always think of urban designers as having the answers. Community demands for new housing that remains part of the neighborhood rather than obliterating it; demands for the preservation of old buildings; regulations requiring Environmental Impact Statements; the concept of joint development for major transportation projects; the general realization that land-use regulations are a strong determinant of city design—all these represent favorable developments for the future of urban design.

Successful design initiatives have awakened real estate interests to the possibility that some things are possible with the cooperation of government that would not be possible for the entrepreneur alone. This is a favorable circumstance as long as the resulting development remains in the public interest.

Another favorable circumstance for urban design is that there is more "patient money" around. Changing tax laws and other business conditions are making it more profitable to hold on to new developments, rather than selling them as soon as they are rented, or as soon as a maximum depreciation has been achieved for tax purposes. There is quite a difference in what developers expect from a project if they plan to hold it rather than sell it off immediately.

The future of the urban designer lies with those governmental authorities that have the power to make large-scale decisions about the environment, and in those businesses and industries whose activities have a big impact on our physical surroundings.

To put it another way, the same institutions that have been the "bad guys" in the design of cities have the greatest capacity to be the "good guys."

Such a transformation almost certainly has to begin

Urban Design: A Process and a Partnership

at the top. The success of day-to-day activities depends on the people doing the work, but major innovations are almost impossible in large institutions unless the leadership is in favor of change.

If the heads of major insurance companies were to make some urban design criteria the conditions for giving permanent financing, they could change the face of cities all over the nation. Civic action by business groups and citizen groups also can make a major difference, and, as local government is so important to urban design, the support of mayors and city managers is essential.

In the end, better urban design will be achieved by a partnership between private investment and government, and between the design professional and the concerned decisionmaker in either private or public life.

The experiences described in this book represent a sample of what urban design can accomplish. But much remains to be learned and much remains to be done.

Acknowledgments

I would like to express my appreciation to William Salo for convincing me that I should write this book; to Barbaralee Diamonstein for a timely introduction and for helpful suggestions about the manuscript; and to Jaquelin Robertson for going over the manuscript and giving useful advice. I also much appreciate the help of the people at Harper & Row: Cass Canfield, Jr., an unfailing encouraging editor; Carol Edwards, a patient and perfectionist production editor; C. Linda Dingler, the graphic designer, who put up with a lot of backseat driving; and others on the editorial staff who had to cope with an author who did things like change the order of chapters at the last moment.

Illustration Credits

71	Drawing and photograph courtesy Fisher-Friedman Associates.
73	Drawing by Le Corbusier from Frederick Etchell's translation of *Towards a New Architecture,* John Rodker edition.
76, 78	Drawings used by permission of the City of New York.
79	Photograph by Norman McGrath courtesy of Der Scutt.
80, 82, 85, 86 87	Drawings used by permission of the City of New York
88	Drawing used by permission of the City of New York, photography by Edmund Stoecklein.
90, 92, 93, 94 95, 96, 98	Drawings used by permission of the City of New York.
104	Model photograph of IBM Building by Louis Checkman, courtesy of Edward L. Barnes; model photographs of A.T.&T. Building by Harr, Hedrich-Blessing courtesy of Johnson/Burgee; model photograph of 499 Park Avenue by Nathaniel Lieberman, courtesy of I. M. Pei & Partners
105	Model photograph and drawing courtesy of Ulrich Franzen & Associates.
106	Photograph by Edmund Stoecklein.
109	Photograph of Lincoln Square Special District by Edmund Stoecklein; photograph of Olympic Tower by Bo Parker courtesy of Skidmore, Owings & Merrill.
110	Photograph by Edmund Stoecklein.
111	Model photograph and drawing courtesy of John Portman and Associates.
113, 114, 115	Drawings used by permission of the City of New York.
116, 117, 118 119	Drawings from the plan for Battery Park City by Alexander Cooper & Associates.
120	Model photograph by Kenneth Champlin, drawing by Ann Marie Baranowski, Cesar Pelli & Associates.

121	Model photograph by Kenneth Champlin.
122, 123	Drawings from the 42nd Street Development Plan by Cooper-Eckstut Associates
124	Model photograph by William A. McDonough courtesy of Eisenman/Robertson architects.
127	Photograph by Jerry Spearman, courtesy of John Portman & Associates.
128, 129, 130 131, 132, 133	Drawings and photographs from the San Francisco Urban Design Plan.
139	Drawings courtesy of *The Architectual Record.*
141	Drawings from the Plan for Pontchartrain by Wallace, McHarg, Roberts & Todd.
142	Diagrams from *Garden Cities of Tomorrow* by Ebenezer Howard.
143, 145	Maps from *The Regional Survey of New York City and Its Environs,* Volume VIII, used by permission of the Regional Plan Association.
144, 145	Drawings courtesy of *The Architectural Record.*
146, 147	Drawings from the Plan for Pontchartrain by Wallace, McHarg, Roberts & Todd.
151	Drawings from the development controls for Shahestan Pahlavi, courtesy of Jaquelin T. Robertson.
152	Drawings by David Crane & Partners courtesy of *The Architectural Record.*
156, 158, 159	Drawings and Joshua Freiwald photographs courtesy of Fisher-Friedman Associates.
160, 161	Drawing and photograph courtesy of Milo Thompson Frederick Bentz.
162	Map from *Les Promenades de Paris* by Adolphe Alphand.
163	Photograph from *Shepp's Photographs of the World.*
164	Drawing from The Plan for Chicago from *The Study of Architectural Design* by John F. Harbeson.
165	From Le Corbusier, *Oeuvre Complète,* by permission of the publishers, Artemis Verlag.

166, 167	Drawing and photographs courtesy of Victor Gruen Associates.
168, 169	Drawings and photograph courtesy of the German Information Service.
170	Photograph by Paul Ryan, courtesy of Lawrence Halprin & Associates.
171	Drawing and photograph courtesy of Lawrence Halprin & Associates.
172	Drawing from *Alleys, A Hidden Resource,* used by permission of Grady Clay and Company; drawing of Adelaide street improvement courtesy of Llewelyn-Davies Kinhill.
173	Drawings from The San Francisco Urban Design Plan.
174, 175	Drawings and photographs courtesy of Lawrence Halpin & Associates.
176, 177	Drawing and photograph courtesy of M. Paul Friedberg & Partners; photograph courtesy of Frederick Bentz/Milo Thompson & Associates, Inc.
178, 179	Drawings used by permission of the City of New York.
180	Map from Minneapolis Metro Center 85.
181	Photograph by Richard Payne, AIA courtesy of Johnson/Burgee.
182	Photographs by Norman McGrath courtesy of Hugh Stubbins & Associates.
183	Drawing courtesy of Hugh Stubbins & Associates.
184, 185	Drawing by Peter Polites courtesy of John Portman & Associates.
186	Photograph by Joshua Freiwald.
191, 192, 193	Drawings by Fred Swiss courtesy of the Pittsburgh City Planning Department.
194	Photograph by Ben-Ami Friedman & Associates.
195, 196	Drawings by Ben-Ami Friedman & Associates.
198	Photograph by Joshua Freiwald.

200	Drawings from the Denver RTD study by Wallace, McHarg, Roberts & Todd.
203	Photograph courtesy of General Motors.
207	Drawings used by permission of the City of New York.
209, 210, 211	Drawings from the Westway Environmental Impact Statement.
212	Photograph by Ben-Ami Friedman & Associates.
215, 217	Drawings and model photographs courtesy of Johnson/Burgee.
219, 221	Drawings from the New York City Housing Quality Study.
224	Map from the 1965/1975 General Plan for the City of Boston.
225, 226	Photograph and drawing courtesy of Frederick Bentz/Milo Thompson & Associates, Inc.
228	Photograph by Steven R. Krog courtesy of the New York State Urban Development Corporation.
229	Photograph courtesy of the New York State Urban Development Corporation.
234	Drawing courtesy of I. M. Pei & Partners.
235	Photograph by Aerial Photo of New England, Inc., courtesy of I. M. Pei & Partners.

Index

Page numbers in italic refer to illustrations.